CASSEROLES

PASTA • VEGETABLES • POTATOES • CHICKEN • MEAT • FISH

STERLING
New York

contents

The oven temperatures in this book are for conventional ovens; if you have a fan-forced oven, decrease the oven temperature by 10-20 degrees.

pasta

carbonara gnocchi bake

1 tablespoon olive oil
1 medium onion, chopped finely
3 cloves garlic, crushed
4 rindless bacon slices, chopped coarsely
1½ cups cream
1 pound potato gnocchi
2 egg yolks
⅔ cup finely grated parmesan cheese
½ cup stale coarse breadcrumbs

1 Preheat oven to 400°F. Oil deep 6-cup ovenproof dish.
2 Heat oil in large frying pan; cook onion, garlic and bacon, stirring, until onion softens and bacon is crisp. Add cream; simmer, uncovered, about 5 minutes or until sauce thickens slightly. Season to taste. Cool.
3 Meanwhile, cook gnocchi in large saucepan of boiling water until tender; drain.
4 Combine gnocchi, sauce, egg yolks and half the cheese in large bowl; pour mixture into dish. Sprinkle with combined remaining cheese and breadcrumbs. Cover dish with foil; bake 25 minutes. Uncover; bake about 15 minutes or until browned.

prep + cook time 55 minutes **serves** 4
nutritional count per serving 59.2g total fat (33.2g saturated fat); 840 cal; 47.3g carbohydrate; 28.6g protein; 4.3g fiber

serving suggestion Serve with crusty bread and a leafy green salad.

seafood mornay lasagnas

6 lasagna sheets
2 ounces butter
⅓ cup plain (all-purpose) flour
2 cups milk
½ cup dry white wine
2 teaspoons finely grated lemon rind
¼ cup finely chopped fresh flat-leaf parsley
6½ ounces uncooked medium shrimp
6½ ounces firm white fish fillets
8½ ounces crab meat
½ cup finely grated parmesan cheese

1 Preheat oven to 425°F. Oil six 1¼-cup ovenproof dishes.
2 Cook lasagna sheets, in batches, in large saucepan of boiling water until tender; drain. Cut each sheet into three squares.
3 Meanwhile, melt butter in large saucepan. Add flour; cook, stirring, about 2 minutes or until mixture bubbles and thickens. Gradually stir in milk and wine. Cook, stirring, until sauce boils and thickens; cool. Stir in rind and parsley; season to taste.
4 Shell and devein shrimp; cut shrimp and fish into ½-inch pieces. Combine seafood in medium bowl.
5 Line base of each dish with one piece of lasagna. Top each with half the seafood, one-third of the sauce, then another piece of lasagna. Top each with remaining seafood, half the remaining sauce and another lasagna sheet. Top each with remaining sauce; sprinkle with cheese. Bake about 15 minutes or until seafood is cooked.

prep + cook time 45 minutes serves 6
nutritional count per serving 15.1g total fat (9.3g saturated fat); 372 cal; 30.6g carbohydrate; 25.1g protein; 1.4g fiber

notes Use fresh, instant or dried lasagna for this recipe. We used larger dishes here – each will serve three.

arugula and spaghetti frittata

6½ ounces spaghetti
8 ounces arugula, chopped coarsely
2 tablespoons roasted pine nuts
¼ cup finely grated parmesan cheese
2 teaspoons finely grated lemon rind
2 cloves garlic, quartered
2 tablespoons olive oil
⅓ cup sun-dried tomatoes in oil, drained, chopped finely
6 eggs
1 cup cream

1 Preheat oven to 400°F. Oil deep 7½-inch square cake pan; line base and sides with parchment paper, extending paper 2 inches over sides. Or, oil deep ovenproof frying pan with base measuring 8 inches.
2 Cook pasta in large saucepan of boiling water until tender; drain.
3 Meanwhile, blend or process arugula, nuts, cheese, rind, garlic and oil until pesto is smooth.
4 Combine pasta, pesto and tomato in large bowl; season to taste. Spread mixture into pan. Whisk eggs and cream in large bowl until combined; pour over pasta mixture. Bake frittata, uncovered, about 35 minutes or until set. Stand frittata in pan 5 minutes before cutting.

prep + cook time 55 minutes **serves** 6
nutritional count per serving 35.1g total fat (15.4g saturated fat); 492 cal; 28.2g carbohydrate; 15.1g protein; 3.4g fiber

serving suggestion Serve with a garden salad.

spaghetti rosa bake

8 ounces spaghetti
1 tablespoon olive oil
1 medium onion, chopped finely
2 cloves garlic, crushed
2⅔ cups bottled tomato sauce
2 tablespoons finely chopped fresh basil
½ cup cream
1½ cups coarsely grated
   mozzarella cheese

1 Preheat oven to 400°F. Oil shallow 8-cup ovenproof dish.
2 Cook pasta in large saucepan of boiling water until tender; drain.
3 Meanwhile, heat oil in large saucepan; cook onion and garlic, stirring, until onion softens. Add sauce and basil; bring to the boil. Reduce heat; simmer, uncovered, about 10 minutes or until sauce is thickened slightly. Stir in cream; season.
4 Stir pasta and half the cheese into hot sauce in pan; spread mixture into dish. Sprinkle with remaining cheese. Bake about 20 minutes or until browned lightly.

prep + cook time 40 minutes **serves** 6
nutritional count per serving 19.9g total fat (10.1g saturated fat); 399 cal; 39.4g carbohydrate; 13.9g protein; 4.5g fiber

penne arrabbiata bake

9½ ounces penne pasta
1 tablespoon olive oil
1 medium onion, chopped finely
3 cloves garlic, crushed
1 fresh long red chili, chopped finely
6 drained anchovy fillets, chopped finely
2 tablespoons finely chopped fresh basil
2⅔ cups bottled tomato pasta sauce
½ cup seeded black olives, chopped coarsely
½ cup pizza cheese

1 Preheat oven to 350°F. Oil deep 8-cup ovenproof dish.
2 Cook pasta in large saucepan of boiling water until tender; drain.
3 Meanwhile, heat oil in large saucepan; cook onion, garlic, chili, anchovy and basil, stirring, until onion softens. Add sauce; bring to the boil. Remove from heat; stir pasta and olives into hot sauce. Season to taste.
4 Spoon mixture into dish; sprinkle with cheese. Bake about 25 minutes or until browned lightly.

prep + cook time 45 minutes **serves** 4
nutritional count per serving 12g total fat (3.1g saturated fat); 473 cal; 70.1g carbohydrate; 17.5g protein; 7.5g fiber

11

This recipe uses four lasagna sheets but only has three pasta layers. We used the fourth sheet to trim and fill any gaps in each pasta layer.

tomato, beef and pea lasagna

1 tablespoon olive oil
1 medium onion, chopped finely
2 cloves garlic, crushed
1 pound ground beef
1½ pounds canned diced tomatoes
½ cup beef stock
¼ cup tomato paste
2 tablespoons finely chopped fresh basil
1 cup frozen peas
2 ounces butter
⅓ cup plain (all-purpose) flour
3 cups hot milk
1½ cups pizza cheese
4 fresh lasagna sheets

1 Heat oil in large frying pan; cook onion and garlic, stirring, until onion softens. Add beef; cook, stirring, until browned. Add undrained tomatoes, stock, paste and basil; bring to the boil. Reduce heat; simmer, covered, 30 minutes. Uncover; simmer, about 10 minutes or until sauce thickens slightly. Stir in peas; season to taste.
2 Meanwhile, melt butter in large saucepan. Add flour; cook, stirring, about 2 minutes or until mixture bubbles and thickens. Gradually stir in milk; cook, stirring, until sauce boils and thickens. Remove from heat; stir in half the cheese.
3 Preheat oven to 400°F. Oil deep 14-cup ovenproof dish.
4 Line base of dish with lasagna sheets, trimming to fit. Top with half the beef mixture, one-third of the cheese sauce, then more lasagna sheets, trimming to fit. Top with remaining beef mixture, half the remaining cheese sauce and remaining lasagna sheets, trimming to fit. Top with remaining cheese sauce; sprinkle with remaining cheese.
5 Cover lasagna with foil; bake 35 minutes. Uncover; bake about 20 minutes or until browned lightly. Stand lasagna 10 minutes before serving.

prep + cook time 1 hour 30 minutes **serves** 8
nutritional count per serving 19.2g total fat (11.5g saturated fat); 366 cal; 22g carbohydrate; 25.3g protein; 3.6g fiber

asparagus, egg and bacon bake

8 ounces penne pasta
1 tablespoon olive oil
1 medium onion, chopped finely
3 cloves garlic, crushed
3 rindless bacon slices, sliced thinly
9½ ounces asparagus, trimmed, chopped coarsely
2 tablespoons plain (all-purpose) flour
½ cup dry white wine
½ cup chicken stock
1 cup cream
4 hard-boiled eggs, quartered
2 tablespoons finely chopped fresh chives
1 cup finely grated parmesan cheese
⅓ cup breadcrumbs

1 Preheat oven to 425°F. Oil deep 10-cup ovenproof dish.
2 Cook pasta in large saucepan of boiling water until tender; drain.
3 Meanwhile, heat oil in large saucepan; cook onion, garlic and bacon, stirring, until bacon is crisp. Add asparagus; cook, stirring, until tender. Add flour; cook, stirring, about 2 minutes or until mixture bubbles and thickens. Gradually stir in wine, stock and cream. Cook, stirring, until mixture boils and thickens.
4 Stir pasta, eggs, chives and half the cheese into asparagus mixture; season to taste. Spoon mixture into dish; sprinkle with combined remaining cheese and breadcrumbs. Bake about 20 minutes or until browned lightly.

prep + cook time 45 minutes **serves** 6
nutritional count per serving 32.6g total fat (17.4g saturated fat); 561 cal; 37.8g carbohydrate; 24.6g protein; 3.1g fiber

pumpkin, spinach and ricotta cannelloni

12½ ounces pumpkin, chopped coarsely
6½ ounces frozen spinach, thawed
6½ ounces ricotta cheese
12 cannelloni tubes
2⅔ cups bottled tomato sauce
½ cup coarsely grated cheddar cheese
½ cup finely grated parmesan cheese

1 Preheat oven to 400°F. Oil shallow 6-cup ovenproof dish.
2 Boil, steam or microwave pumpkin until tender; drain. Mash pumpkin in medium bowl until smooth; cool.
3 Squeeze excess liquid from spinach; chop coarsely. Stir spinach and ricotta into pumpkin; season to taste. Fill cannelloni tubes with pumpkin mixture.
4 Spread half the sauce over base of dish; top with cannelloni, in single layer. Pour remaining sauce over cannelloni; sprinkle with combined cheddar and parmesan.
5 Cover dish with foil; bake 35 minutes. Uncover; bake about 20 minutes or until cannelloni are tender and cheese is browned lightly.

prep + cook time 1 hour 20 minutes **serves** 4
nutritional count per serving 17.8g total fat (9.5g saturated fat); 457 cal; 46.3g carbohydrate; 23.7g protein; 9g fiber

serving suggestion Serve with a leafy green salad.
note We used butternut pumpkin for this recipe.

spinach and ricotta pasta slice

9½ ounces angel hair pasta
13 ounces canned tomato puree
4½ ounces baby spinach leaves
9½ ounces ricotta cheese
4 eggs
½ cup cream
½ cup pizza cheese

1 Preheat oven to 400°F. Oil shallow 8-cup ovenproof dish.
2 Cook pasta in large saucepan of boiling water until tender; drain, cool.
3 Spread one-third of the tomato puree over base of dish; top with half the spinach, half the pasta and half the ricotta. Pour half the remaining tomato puree over ricotta; top with remaining spinach and remaining pasta. Pour remaining tomato puree over pasta; sprinkle with remaining ricotta.
4 Whisk eggs and cream in large bowl until combined; season. Pour egg mixture over pasta; sprinkle with pizza cheese. Bake, uncovered, about 40 minutes or until browned lightly and set.

prep + cook time 1 hour serves 6
nutritional count per serving 20.9g total fat (12g saturated fat); 431 cal; 39.1g carbohydrate; 19.9g protein; 3.6g fiber

broccoli and cheese penne with garlic and lemon crumbs

6½ ounces penne pasta
1 pound broccoli, cut into small florets
3 eggs
1 cup cream
⅓ cup milk
⅔ cup coarsely grated cheddar cheese
½ cup breadcrumbs
1 cup finely grated parmesan cheese
2 cloves garlic, crushed
1 tablespoon finely grated lemon rind
2 tablespoons finely chopped fresh flat-leaf parsley

1 Preheat oven to 425°F. Oil deep 8-cup ovenproof dish.
2 Cook pasta in large saucepan of boiling water until tender. Add broccoli for last 5 minutes of pasta cooking time; drain. Rinse pasta and broccoli under cold water; drain, cool.
3 Combine pasta, broccoli, eggs, cream, milk and cheddar in large bowl; season. Spoon mixture into dish; sprinkle with combined breadcrumbs, parmesan, garlic, rind and parsley. Bake, uncovered, about 40 minutes or until browned lightly and set. Stand 10 minutes before serving.

prep + cook time 1 hour serves 6
nutritional count per serving 30.5g total fat (18.8g saturated fat); 490 cal; 29.3g carbohydrate; 21.6g protein; 5.1g fiber

pastitsio

1 tablespoon olive oil
1 medium onion, chopped finely
2 cloves garlic, crushed
1 pound ground beef
1 teaspoon ground cinnamon
½ teaspoon ground nutmeg
1½ pounds canned diced tomatoes
½ cup dry white wine
½ cup beef stock
¼ cup tomato paste
2 tablespoons finely chopped fresh flat-leaf parsley
6½ ounces macaroni pasta
1 egg
1 cup finely grated parmesan cheese
¼ cup breadcrumbs

CHEESE TOPPING
2 ounces butter
⅓ cup plain (all-purpose) flour
2 cups hot milk
1 cup finely grated parmesan cheese
1 egg yolk

1 Heat oil in large frying pan; cook onion and garlic, stirring, until onion softens. Add beef and spices; cook, stirring, until browned and fragrant. Add undrained tomatoes, wine, stock and paste; bring to the boil. Reduce heat; simmer, covered, 30 minutes. Uncover; simmer, about 5 minutes or until sauce thickens slightly. Stir in parsley; season to taste.
2 Meanwhile, make cheese topping.
3 Preheat oven to 400°F. Oil shallow 8-cup ovenproof dish.
4 Cook pasta in large saucepan of boiling water until tender; drain. Combine pasta and egg in large bowl. Spoon pasta mixture into dish; top with beef mixture. Spread cheese topping over beef mixture; sprinkle with combined cheese and breadcrumbs. Bake, uncovered, about 25 minutes or until browned lightly. Stand 5 minutes before serving.

CHEESE TOPPING Melt butter in medium saucepan. Add flour; cook, stirring, about 2 minutes or until mixture bubbles and thickens. Gradually stir in milk; cook, stirring, until sauce boils and thickens. Remove from heat; stir in cheese and egg yolk.

prep + cook time 1 hour 30 minutes serves 6
nutritional count per serving 32.2g total fat (17.3g saturated fat); 631 cal; 41.7g carbohydrate; 38.4g protein; 4.2g fiber

classic macaroni cheese

12 ounces macaroni pasta
2 ounces butter
¼ cup plain (all-purpose) flour
3 cups hot milk
1½ cups coarsely grated cheddar cheese
1 cup coarse white breadcrumbs

1   Preheat oven to 350°F. Oil 6-cup ovenproof dish.
2   Cook pasta in large saucepan of boiling water until tender; drain.

3   Meanwhile, melt butter in large saucepan. Add flour; cook, stirring, about 2 minutes or until mixture bubbles and thickens. Gradually stir in milk. Cook, stirring, until sauce boils and thickens. Stir in 1 cup of the cheese.
4   Stir pasta into hot sauce mixture; spoon into dish. Sprinkle with combined breadcrumbs and remaining cheese. Bake, uncovered, about 25 minutes or until browned lightly.

prep + cook time 1 hour **serves** 4
nutritional count per serving 36.5g total fat (22.9g saturated fat); 821 cal; 89.7g carbohydrate; 31.5g protein; 4.1g fiber

note We used ciabatta bread to make the breadcrumbs.

tuna mornay with pasta

12 ounces elbow pasta
2 ounces butter
1 medium onion, chopped finely
1 clove garlic, crushed
2 stalks celery, trimmed, chopped finely
¼ cup plain (all-purpose) flour
1½ cups hot milk
1 cup cream
13½ ounces canned tuna in springwater, drained, flaked
2 tablespoons finely chopped fresh flat-leaf parsley
2 teaspoons finely grated lemon rind
1 cup coarse breadcrumbs
1 cup coarsely grated cheddar cheese

1 Preheat oven to 350°F. Oil deep 10-cup ovenproof dish.
2 Cook pasta in large saucepan of boiling water until tender; drain.
3 Melt butter in large saucepan; cook onion, garlic and celery, stirring, until onion softens. Add flour; cook, stirring, about 2 minutes or until mixture bubbles and thickens. Gradually stir in milk and cream. Cook, stirring, until sauce boils and thickens.
4 Stir pasta, tuna, parsley and rind into sauce mixture; season. Spoon mixture into dish; sprinkle with combined breadcrumbs and cheese. Bake, uncovered, about 35 minutes or until browned lightly.

prep + cook time 1 hour **serves** 6
nutritional count per serving 38g total fat (24g saturated fat); 717 cal; 61.1g carbohydrate; 31g protein; 3.8g fiber

creamy bolognese pasta bake

1 tablespoon olive oil
1 medium onion, chopped finely
3 cloves garlic, crushed
2 stalks celery, trimmed, chopped finely
1 large carrot, chopped finely
1 pound ground beef
½ cup dry red wine
½ cup beef stock
13 ounces canned diced tomatoes
⅓ cup tomato paste
1 cup milk
½ cup frozen peas
¼ cup finely chopped fresh flat-leaf parsley
9½ ounces rigatoni pasta
1½ cups coarsely grated cheddar cheese

1 Heat oil in large saucepan; cook onion, garlic, celery and carrot, stirring, until vegetables soften. Add beef; cook, stirring, until browned. Add wine; bring to the boil. Boil, uncovered, until liquid is almost evaporated. Add stock, undrained tomatoes, paste and milk; bring to the boil. Reduce heat; simmer, uncovered, about 30 minutes or until sauce thickens slightly. Stir in peas and parsley; season to taste.

2 Preheat oven to 425°F. Oil deep 12-cup ovenproof dish.

3 Cook pasta in large saucepan of boiling water until tender; drain.

4 Stir pasta into bolognese mixture with half the cheese. Spoon mixture into dish; sprinkle with remaining cheese. Bake, uncovered, about 15 minutes or until browned lightly. Stand 5 minutes before serving.

prep + cook time 1 hour 10 minutes **serves** 6
nutritional count per serving 22g total fat (11.2g saturated fat); 537 cal; 44.2g carbohydrate; 34g protein; 5.8g fiber

vegetables

spinach and sweet potato gnocchi

2 pounds sweet potato, chopped coarsely
2 medium russet potatoes, chopped coarsely
½ cup finely chopped spinach leaves
1 cup plain (all-purpose) flour, approximately
½ cup finely grated parmesan cheese

TOMATO BASIL SAUCE
1 tablespoon olive oil
1 small brown onion, chopped finely
2 cloves garlic, crushed
4 medium tomatoes, chopped finely
¼ cup finely chopped fresh basil

1 Preheat oven to 400°F. Oil six shallow 1½-cup ovenproof dishes.
2 Roast sweet potato and russet potato, in single layer, on oiled oven tray, about 40 minutes or until tender; cool.
3 Meanwhile, make tomato basil sauce.
4 Push sweet potato and russet potato through potato ricer or sieve into large bowl. Stir in spinach and enough of the sifted flour to make a soft, sticky dough.
5 To make gnocchi flatten dough on floured surface to ½-inch thickness. Cut 2-inch rounds from dough; transfer gnocchi to tea-towel-lined tray. Reshape and cut rounds from any remaining dough until all dough is used.
6 Cook gnocchi, in batches, in large saucepan of boiling water until gnocchi float to the surface and are cooked through. Remove gnocchi using slotted spoon; transfer to dishes. Top with sauce, sprinkle with cheese. Bake, uncovered, about 15 minutes or until browned lightly.

TOMATO BASIL SAUCE Heat oil in medium saucepan; cook onion and garlic, stirring, until onion softens. Add tomato; cook, stirring, about 5 minutes or until tomato softens. Simmer, uncovered, 10 minutes or until sauce thickens slightly. Stir in basil; season to taste.

prep + cook time 1 hour 30 minutes serves 6
nutritional count per serving 5.8g total fat (1.9g saturated fat); 295 cal; 46.6g carbohydrate; 10.4g protein; 5.9g fiber

note You will need to buy one bunch of spinach (9½ ounces) to make this recipe.

curried lentil pies

2 tablespoons ghee
1 medium onion, chopped finely
2 cloves garlic, crushed
1½-inch piece fresh ginger, grated
1 fresh long red chili, chopped finely
1 stalk celery, trimmed, chopped coarsely
1 large carrot, chopped coarsely
2 teaspoons each black mustard seeds, ground cumin
   and ground cilantro
1 teaspoon ground turmeric
1½ cups brown lentils
13 ounces canned crushed tomatoes
2 cups vegetable stock
⅔ cup coconut milk
½ cup frozen peas
½ cup coarsely chopped fresh cilantro
1¼ pounds pumpkin, chopped coarsely
2 medium potatoes, chopped coarsely
2 ounces butter

1 Heat ghee in large saucepan; cook onion, garlic, ginger, chili, celery and carrot, stirring, until vegetables soften. Add spices; cook, stirring, until fragrant. Add lentils, undrained tomatoes and stock; simmer, covered, stirring occasionally, about 1 hour or until lentils are tender. Stir in coconut milk, peas and cilantro; season to taste.

2 Meanwhile, boil, steam or microwave pumpkin and potato until tender; drain. Mash pumpkin and potato with butter in medium bowl until smooth.

3 Preheat oven to 425°F. Oil four deep 1¼-cup ovenproof dishes.

4 Divide lentil mixture among dishes; top with pumpkin mixture. Bake, uncovered, about 20 minutes or until browned lightly. Sprinkle with black sesame seeds if you like.

prep + cook time 1 hour serves 4
nutritional count per serving 31.9g total fat (21.7g saturated fat); 669 cal; 60.3g carbohydrate; 28.3g protein; 18.9g fiber

eggplant parmigiana

2 medium eggplants
2 teaspoons coarse cooking (kosher) salt
1 tablespoon olive oil
1 medium onion, chopped finely
2 cloves garlic, crushed
2 tablespoons finely chopped fresh basil
2⅔ cups bottled tomato sauce
1½ cups coarsely grated mozzarella cheese
½ cup finely grated parmesan cheese
½ cup coarse breadcrumbs

1 Peel and discard strips of skin from eggplant; cut eggplant into ¼-inch slices. Place eggplant in colander; sprinkle with salt. Stand in sink 30 minutes. Rinse eggplant under cold water; drain. Squeeze excess water from eggplant.
2 Meanwhile, heat oil in medium saucepan; cook onion, garlic and basil, stirring, until onion softens. Add sauce; bring to the boil. Reduce heat; simmer, uncovered, about 15 minutes or until sauce thickens slightly. Season to taste.
3 Preheat oven to 425°F. Oil six 1¼-cup ovenproof dishes.
4 Spoon half the sauce into dishes; top with half the eggplant and half the mozzarella. Top with remaining eggplant, remaining sauce, then remaining mozzarella. Sprinkle with combined parmesan and breadcrumbs.
5 Cover dishes with foil; place on oven tray. Bake about 40 minutes or until eggplant is tender. Uncover; bake about 15 minutes or until browned lightly.

prep + cook time 1 hour 15 minutes serves 6
nutritional count per serving 13.2g total fat (5.5g saturated fat); 249 cal; 16.9g carbohydrate; 13.4g protein; 5.6g fiber

note We've used larger dishes here – each dish will serve three.

root vegetable gratin

2 medium potatoes
2 medium carrots
2 medium parsnips
1 small brown onion
⅔ cup cream
⅔ cup milk
2 tablespoons finely chopped fresh flat-leaf parsley
1 tablespoon horseradish cream
⅓ cup breadcrumbs

1 Preheat oven to 400°F. Oil deep 6-cup ovenproof dish.
2 Using mandolin or V-slicer, cut potato, carrot, parsnip and onion into paper-thin slices. Place potato over base of dish; top with half the onion. Top with carrot, then remaining onion and parsnip.
3 Combine cream, milk, parsley and horseradish cream in large bowl; season. Pour cream mixture over vegetables; sprinkle with breadcrumbs.
4 Cover dish with foil; bake about 1¼ hours or until vegetables are tender. Uncover; bake about 30 minutes or until browned lightly. Stand 5 minutes before serving.

prep + cook time 2 hours **serves** 4
nutritional count per serving 20g total fat (12.8g saturated fat); 358 cal; 33.8g carbohydrate; 7.8g protein; 6.3g fiber

cheese and vegetable polenta bake

1½ ounces butter
1 medium onion, chopped finely
1 clove garlic, crushed
1 medium eggplant, chopped finely
1 medium red bell pepper, chopped finely
1 medium green bell pepper, chopped finely
3 ounces button mushrooms, chopped finely
13 ounces canned crushed tomatoes
2 tablespoons finely chopped fresh basil
4 cups water
1⅓ cups polenta
½ cup finely grated parmesan cheese
½ cup coarsely grated cheddar cheese

1 Preheat oven to 425°F. Oil deep 7-cup ovenproof dish.
2 Melt butter in large frying pan; cook onion and garlic, stirring, until onion softens. Add eggplant, peppers, mushrooms and undrained tomatoes; bring to the boil. Reduce heat; simmer, uncovered, about 15 minutes or until vegetables are tender and sauce thickens slightly. Remove from heat; stir in basil. Season to taste.
3 Meanwhile, bring the water to the boil in medium saucepan; gradually stir in polenta. Cook, stirring, about 5 minutes or until polenta thickens. Stir in cheeses; season to taste.
4 Spread half the polenta mixture over base of dish; top with vegetable mixture. Spread remaining polenta mixture over vegetables. Bake about 20 minutes or until browned lightly. Stand 5 minutes before serving.

prep + cook time 55 minutes **serves** 4
nutritional count per serving 19.3g total fat (11.5g saturated fat); 449 cal; 49g carbohydrate; 16.6g protein; 6.5g fiber

veggie casserole with chive dumplings

1 tablespoon olive oil
1 large leek, sliced thinly
2 cloves garlic, crushed
3 rindless bacon slices, chopped coarsely
2 stalks celery, trimmed, chopped coarsely
1 large carrot, chopped coarsely
2 medium red bell peppers, chopped coarsely
2 medium zucchini, chopped coarsely
½ cup dry red wine
13 ounces canned crushed tomatoes
1 cup water
12½ ounces swiss brown mushrooms, halved
½ cup frozen peas

CHIVE DUMPLINGS
1½ cups self-raising flour
2 ounces butter, chopped finely
¾ cup finely grated parmesan cheese
2 tablespoons finely chopped fresh chives
½ cup milk, approximately

1 Preheat oven to 350°F.
2 Heat oil in large flameproof casserole dish; cook leek, garlic and bacon, stirring, until leek softens and bacon is crisp. Add celery, carrot, peppers, zucchini, wine, undrained tomatoes and the water; bring to the boil. Cover; bake about 20 minutes or until vegetables are tender.
3 Meanwhile, make chive dumplings.
4 Remove dish from oven; stir in mushrooms and peas. Season. Drop level tablespoons of dumpling mixture on top of stew.
5 Bake, uncovered, about 20 minutes or until dumplings are puffed and browned lightly.

CHIVE DUMPLINGS Sift flour into medium bowl; rub in butter. Stir in cheese and chives, then enough milk to make a soft sticky dough.

prep + cook time 45 minutes serves 6
nutritional count per serving 19.6g total fat (9.6g saturated fat); 457 cal; 39.8g carbohydrate; 22g protein; 9.9g fiber

pumpkin, pea and feta risotto

1 pound pumpkin, chopped coarsely
1 tablespoon olive oil
2 cups chicken stock
2 cups water
1 medium onion, chopped finely
2 cloves garlic, crushed
1½ cups arborio rice
8 ounces grape tomatoes
1 cup frozen peas
⅓ cup finely grated parmesan cheese
3 ounces soft feta cheese, crumbled
1 tablespoon coarsely chopped fresh marjoram

1 Preheat oven to 425°F.
2 Combine pumpkin and half the oil in medium shallow flameproof casserole dish. Roast, uncovered, about 20 minutes or until tender; remove from dish.
3 Reduce oven to 350°F.
4 Bring stock and the water to the boil in medium saucepan. Reduce heat; simmer, covered.
5 Meanwhile, heat remaining oil in same dish; cook onion and garlic, stirring, until onion softens. Add rice; stir to coat in onion mixture. Stir in simmering stock mixture; cover dish with foil.
6 Bake 25 minutes, stirring halfway through cooking time. Remove risotto from oven; stir in tomatoes and peas. Bake, uncovered, about 10 minutes or until rice is tender. Stir in pumpkin and parmesan; season to taste. Sprinkle with feta and marjoram.

prep + cook time 1 hour serves 4
nutritional count per serving 13.9g total fat (6.4g saturated fat); 508 cal; 73.7g carbohydrate; 18.4g protein; 6.1g fiber

cauliflower and broccoli gratin

½ small cauliflower, cut into large florets
12½ ounces broccoli, cut into large florets
2 ounces butter
¼ cup plain (all-purpose) flour
3 cups hot milk
1 cup coarsely grated cheddar cheese
½ cup breadcrumbs
½ cup finely grated parmesan cheese

1 Preheat oven to 425°F. Oil shallow 7-cup ovenproof dish.
2 Boil, steam or microwave cauliflower and broccoli, separately, until tender; drain.
3 Meanwhile, melt butter in large saucepan. Add flour; cook, stirring, about 2 minutes or until mixture bubbles and thickens. Gradually stir in milk; cook, stirring, until sauce boils and thickens. Stir in cheddar; season to taste.
4 Place cauliflower and broccoli in dish, pour cheese sauce over; sprinkle with combined breadcrumbs and parmesan. Bake, uncovered, about 20 minutes or until browned lightly.

prep + cook time 45 minutes **serves** 6 (as a side dish)
nutritional count per serving 22.7g total fat (14.3g saturated fat); 355 cal; 16.4g carbohydrate; 19.1g protein; 5.4g fiber

notes To prevent excess water leaching into the gratin, steaming is the best method to use for cooking the vegetables. You can use broccolini instead of broccoli, if you prefer.
We've used two ovenproof pans here – each pan will serve three.

fennel and leek gratin

4 baby fennel bulbs
1 medium leek, sliced thinly
1½ cups cream
½ cup milk
1½ ounces butter
2 tablespoons plain (all-purpose) flour
⅓ cup coarsely grated cheddar cheese
⅓ cup finely grated parmesan cheese
⅔ cup breadcrumbs

1 Trim and quarter fennel; reserve 1 tablespoon finely chopped fennel fronds.
2 Combine fennel, leek, cream and milk in large saucepan; simmer, covered, about 15 minutes or until fennel is tender. Transfer fennel and leek to six shallow 1-cup ovenproof dishes; reserve cream mixture.
3 Preheat oven to 425°F.
4 Melt butter in same pan. Add flour; cook, stirring, about 2 minutes or until mixture bubbles and thickens. Gradually stir in hot cream mixture. Cook, stirring, until sauce boils and thickens; season to taste.
5 Pour sauce over fennel; sprinkle with combined cheeses, breadcrumbs and reserved fennel fronds. Bake, uncovered, about 15 minutes or until browned lightly.

prep + cook time 45 minutes **serves** 6 (as a side dish)
nutritional count per serving 38.2g total fat (24.8g saturated fat); 440 cal; 15.2g carbohydrate; 8.5g protein; 3.7g fiber

serving suggestion Serve with roast lamb, beef or veal, or your favorite steak.

potatoes

potato gratin with caramelized onion

1 tablespoon olive oil
2 large brown onions, sliced thinly
1 tablespoon light brown sugar
3 teaspoons balsamic vinegar
2 tablespoons coarsely chopped fresh flat-leaf parsley
2 pounds potatoes
1 tablespoon plain (all-purpose) flour
1¾ cups cream
¼ cup milk
¾ ounce butter, chopped finely
¾ cup coarsely grated gruyère cheese
¾ cup breadcrumbs

1 Heat oil in medium frying pan over low heat; cook onion, stirring occasionally, about 20 minutes or until onion softens. Add sugar and vinegar; cook, stirring occasionally, about 10 minutes or until onion is caramelized. Remove from heat; stir in parsley.

2 Preheat oven to 350°F. Oil 6-cup ovenproof dish.

3 Using mandolin or V-slicer, cut potatoes into paper thin slices; pat dry with paper towels. Layer half the potato in dish; top with caramelized onion, then remaining potato.

4 Blend flour with a little of the cream in medium bowl; stir in remaining cream and milk. Pour cream mixture over potato mixture; dot with butter. Cover with foil; bake 1¼ hours. Uncover; sprinkle with combined cheese and breadcrumbs. Bake, uncovered, about 15 minutes or until potato is tender. Stand 5 minutes before serving.

prep + cook time 1 hour 45 minutes **serves** 6
nutritional count per serving 42.1g total fat (25.8g saturated fat); 559 cal; 32.9g carbohydrate; 11.5g protein; 3.5g fiber

note We used sebago potatoes in this recipe.

potatoes with lemon and tomato

2½ pounds medium potatoes, cut into thick wedges
2 medium lemons, sliced thickly
1 tablespoon fresh thyme leaves
½ cup dry white wine
2 tablespoons olive oil
15½ ounces cherry tomatoes, cut into 2-inch lengths
½ cup pitted kalamata olives
2 tablespoons coarsely chopped fresh flat-leaf parsley

1 Preheat oven to 400°F. Oil 10-cup ovenproof dish.
2 Combine potato, lemon and thyme in dish; pour over combined wine and oil. Season. Cover dish with foil; bake 40 minutes. Uncover; bake 30 minutes. Remove from oven; top with tomatoes. Bake, uncovered, further 12 minutes or until potato is tender.
3 Serve sprinkled with olives and parsley.

prep + cook time 1 hour 35 minutes **serves** 6
nutritional count per serving 6.6g total fat (0.9g saturated fat); 903kJ (216 cal); 26.8g carbohydrate; 4.7g protein; 5.2g fiber

serving suggestion Serve with grilled or barbecued chicken or fish.

potato, bacon and blue cheese bake

2½ pounds medium potatoes, sliced thickly
2 medium red onions, cut into thick wedges
10 ounces rindless bacon slices, chopped coarsely
12 sprigs fresh thyme
¾ cup cream
¾ cup salt-reduced chicken stock
4 ounces blue cheese, crumbled

1 Preheat oven to 400°F. Oil 10-cup ovenproof dish.
2 Combine potato, onion and bacon in dish; top with half the thyme. Combine cream and stock in medium bowl; season, pour over potato.
3 Bake, uncovered, about 1½ hours or until potato is tender. Serve topped with cheese and remaining thyme.

prep + cook time 1 hour 45 minutes **serves** 6
nutritional count per serving 22.9g total fat (13.5g saturated fat); 397 cal; 25.6g carbohydrate; 20.5g protein; 3.3g fiber

45

potato gnocchi with three-cheese sauce

1 pound potatoes, unpeeled
1 egg, beaten lightly
½ ounce butter, melted
2 tablespoons finely grated parmesan cheese
1 cup plain (all-purpose) flour, approximately
¼ cup coarse breadcrumbs

THREE-CHEESE SAUCE

1 cup cream
½ cup coarsely grated mozzarella cheese
1½ ounces gorgonzola cheese, crumbled
½ cup finely grated parmesan cheese
1 teaspoon dijon mustard
¼ teaspoon ground nutmeg
1 egg yolk
1 tablespoon finely chopped fresh curly parsley

1 Boil or steam whole potatoes until tender; drain. When cool enough to handle, peel away skins. Mash potatoes, using ricer, food mill (mouli) or strainer, into medium bowl; stir in egg, butter, cheese and enough flour to make a firm dough.
2 Divide dough into four portions; roll each portion on floured surface into ¾ inch thick sausage shape. Cut each sausage into ¾ inch pieces; roll pieces into balls.
3 Roll each ball along the tines of a fork, pressing lightly on top of ball with index finger to form classic gnocchi shape – grooved on one side and dimpled on the other. Place gnocchi, in single layer, on lightly floured tray; cover, refrigerate 1 hour.
4 Meanwhile, make three-cheese sauce.
5 Preheat oven to 425°F. Oil four 8-ounce ovenproof dishes.
6 Cook gnocchi, in batches, in large saucepan of boiling water until gnocchi float to the surface and are cooked through. Remove from pan with slotted spoon; divide among dishes. Pour sauce over gnocchi; sprinkle with breadcrumbs. Bake, uncovered, about 15 minutes.

THREE-CHEESE SAUCE Combine cream and cheeses in small saucepan; stir over medium heat until smooth. Remove from heat; stir in mustard, nutmeg, egg yolk and parsley. Season to taste.

prep + cook time 1 hour (+ refrigeration) serves 4
nutritional count per serving 44.3g total fat (27.8g saturated fat); 607 cal; 33.2g carbohydrate; 19.3g protein; 1.8g fiber

serving suggestion Serve with a green salad.
note We used russet burbank potatoes in this recipe.

mashed potato and bacon bake

4 pounds potatoes, chopped coarsely
13 ounces rindless bacon slices, chopped finely
1 cup sour cream
3 ounces butter, chopped coarsely
¾ cup hot milk
4 scallions, sliced thinly
2 cups coarsely grated cheddar cheese

1 Preheat oven to 350°F. Oil 10-cup ovenproof dish.
2 Boil steam or microwave potato until tender; drain.
3 Meanwhile, cook bacon in large frying pan, stirring, until crisp; drain on paper towel.
4 Mash potato in large bowl with sour cream, butter and milk until smooth. Stir in half the bacon, half the scallion and half the cheese. Season to taste. Spread mixture into dish; sprinkle with remaining bacon, scallion and cheese. Bake, uncovered, about 40 minutes or until browned lightly.

prep + cook time 1 hour 20 minutes **serves** 8
nutritional count per serving 36.9g total fat (22.6g saturated fat); 551 cal; 28.9g carbohydrate; 24.5g protein; 3.3g fiber

potato frittata

2 tablespoons olive oil
1¼ pounds potatoes, chopped coarsely
1½ ounces baby spinach leaves
2 tablespoons coarsely chopped fresh flat-leaf parsley
4 ounces goat's feta cheese, crumbled
⅓ cup coarsely grated parmesan cheese
6 eggs
½ cup cream

1 Preheat oven to 400°F. Oil deep 8-inch square cake pan; line base and sides with parchment paper; extending paper 2 inches over sides. Or, oil deep ovenproof frying pan with base measuring 8 inches.

2 Heat oil in large frying pan; cook potato, stirring, until browned lightly and almost tender. Drain on paper towel.
3 Layer half the spinach, parsley, potato and cheeses in pan; repeat layers. Combine eggs and cream in medium bowl; season. Pour egg mixture into pan. Bake about 30 minutes or until set. Stand 5 minutes before serving.

prep + cook time 50 minutes **serves** 4
nutritional count per serving 39.8g total fat (18.6g saturated fat); 519 cal; 17.8g carbohydrate; 21.7g protein; 2.4g fiber

note We used desiree potatoes in this recipe.

twice-baked potatoes

8 medium potatoes, unpeeled
6½ ounces rindless bacon slices, chopped finely
4 ounces canned creamed corn
¼ cup sour cream
2 scallions, sliced thinly
1 cup coarsely grated cheddar cheese

1 Preheat oven to 350°F.
2 Pierce skin of each potato with a skewer or fork; wrap each potato in foil, place in parchment-paper-lined large shallow baking dish. Bake, uncovered, about 1 hour and 20 minutes or until tender.
3 Meanwhile, cook bacon in medium frying pan until crisp. Drain on paper towel.
4 Cut a shallow slice from each potato; scoop flesh from each top into medium bowl, discard skin. Scoop about two-thirds of the flesh from each potato into same bowl; place potato shells in same baking dish.
5 Mash potato until smooth; stir in creamed corn, sour cream, bacon, half the scallion and half the cheese. Divide mixture into potato shells; sprinkle with remaining scallion and cheese. Bake, uncovered, about 20 minutes or until heated through.

prep + cook time 1 hour 55 minutes **serves** 4
nutritional count per serving 21g total fat (12g saturated fat); 506 cal; 48.3g carbohydrate; 26.6g protein; 6.3g fiber

ham, potato, leek and artichoke bake

1½ ounces butter
 2 tablespoons plain (all-purpose) flour
 2 cups hot chicken stock
 2 pounds potatoes, sliced thickly
 2 medium leeks, sliced thickly
6½ ounces leg ham, chopped coarsely
 9 ounces bottled artichoke hearts in brine,
    drained, halved
 1 cup coarsely grated parmesan cheese

1   Preheat oven to 400°F. Oil 8-cup ovenproof dish.
2   Melt butter in medium saucepan. Add flour; cook, stirring,
about 2 minutes or until mixture bubbles and thickens.
Gradually stir in stock; cook sauce, stirring, until mixture
boils and thickens. Season to taste.
3   Layer half the potato in dish; top with leek, ham, artichokes
and the remaining potato. Pour sauce over potato. Cover
dish with foil; bake 1 hour 20 minutes. Uncover; sprinkle
with cheese. Bake about 30 minutes or until potato is tender.
Stand 10 minutes before serving.

prep + cook time 2 hours **serves** 8
nutritional count per serving 9.6g total fat (5.6g saturated
fat); 232 cal; 19.6g carbohydrate; 14.2g protein; 5.1g fiber

seafood

salmon and zucchini lasagna

1½ ounces butter
¼ cup plain (all-purpose) flour
2 cups hot milk
1 cup ricotta cheese
3 scallions, chopped finely
2 tablespoons finely chopped fresh mint
2 large zucchini, sliced thinly lengthways
3 fresh lasagna sheets
12½ ounces skinless salmon fillet, sliced thinly
½ cup coarsely grated mozzarella cheese

1 Preheat oven to 425°F.
2 Melt butter in medium saucepan. Add flour; cook, stirring, about 2 minutes or until mixture bubbles and thickens. Gradually stir in milk; cook, stirring, until sauce boils and thickens. Season to taste. Spoon 1 cup white sauce into medium bowl; stir in ricotta, scallion and mint.
3 Cook zucchini in large saucepan of boiling, salted water for 2 minutes. Drain zucchini in a single layer on paper towels. Cook pasta, in batches, in same pan of boiling water for about 30 seconds or until tender; drain.
4 Spread ⅓ cup white sauce over base of 4-cup ovenproof dish. Top with a lasagna sheet, half the zucchini, then half the fish and half the ricotta mixture. Repeat layering, seasoning lightly between layers, with remaining lasagna, zucchini, fish and ricotta mixture, finishing with a lasagna sheet. Top with remaining white sauce; sprinkle with mozzarella. Bake, uncovered, about 20 minutes or until browned lightly.

prep + cook time 50 minutes **serves** 4
nutritional count per serving 31.5g total fat (17.1g saturated fat); 608 cal; 40.4g carbohydrate; 39.6g protein; 3.1g fiber

notes To ensure the fish doesn't overcook during the baking time, you need to pre-cook the zucchini and pasta. As cooked, drained lasagna sheets tend to stick together, it's better to cook each sheet just before using it.

tuna and asparagus crumble

1½ ounces butter
2 medium leeks, chopped finely
11 ounces asparagus, chopped coarsely
1 cup cream
13½ ounces canned tuna in water, drained, flaked

CRUMBLE OAT TOPPING
⅔ cup rolled oats
⅓ cup coarsely grated cheddar cheese
2 tablespoons plain (all-purpose) flour
1 ounce butter, chopped finely

1 Make crumble oat topping.
2 Preheat oven to 475°F.
3 Melt butter in large frying pan; cook leek, stirring, 2 minutes. Add asparagus; cook, covered, about 5 minutes or until asparagus is tender. Add cream and tuna; bring to the boil. Season to taste.
4 Spoon mixture into four 1¼-cup ovenproof dishes; sprinkle with topping. Bake about 20 minutes or until browned lightly.

CRUMBLE OAT TOPPING Process ingredients until coarsely chopped.

prep + cook time 45 minutes serves 4
nutritional count per serving 52g total fat (32.5g saturated fat); 696 cal; 23g carbohydrate; 31.5g protein; 8.3g fiber

note We used larger dishes here – each dish will serve two.

salmon, potato and arugula cake

2 pounds potatoes, chopped coarsely
1 cup light sour cream
½ cup cream
2 eggs, beaten lightly
8 ounces arugula, trimmed, chopped coarsely
¾ cup finely grated parmesan cheese
12½ ounces canned red salmon, drained, flaked

1 Preheat oven to 350°F.
2 Boil, steam or microwave potato until tender; drain. Mash potato in large bowl with sour cream and cream until smooth. Stir in egg, arugula and ½ cup of the cheese; season.
3 Divide half the mixture between four 1½-cup ovenproof dishes; top with salmon. Cover salmon with remaining potato mixture; sprinkle with remaining cheese. Bake, uncovered, about 30 minutes or until browned lightly and set.

prep + cook time 1 hour 10 minutes **serves** 4
nutritional count per serving 43.2g total fat (23.3g saturated fat); 666 cal; 31.5g carbohydrate; 36g protein; 4.1g fiber

note We used sebago potatoes in this recipe.

jansson's temptation

3 ounces canned anchovies in oil
1 large onion, sliced thinly
2 pounds potatoes, sliced thinly
1 cup cream
2 tablespoons breadcrumbs
1 ounce butter, chopped finely

1 Preheat oven to 425°F.
2 Drain anchovies over medium frying pan; finely chop anchovies. Heat anchovy oil in pan; cook onion, stirring, until soft.

3 Layer one-third of potato over base of 6-cup ovenproof dish; sprinkle with one-third of the onion and anchovy. Repeat layering with remaining potato, onion and anchovy. Pour over cream; sprinkle with breadcrumbs. Dot with butter.
4 Cover dish loosely with foil; bake about 1 hour or until potato is tender. Uncover; bake about 15 minutes or until browned lightly.

prep + cook time 1 hour 40 minutes **serves** 4
nutritional count per serving 39.3g total fat (22.9g saturated fat);532 cal; 32.6g carbohydrate; 10.6g protein; 4g fiber

creamy fish and potato bake

3 cups milk
3 cloves garlic, crushed
2 pounds potatoes, sliced thinly
1½ ounces butter, chopped finely
2 medium onions, sliced thinly
2 tablespoons plain (all-purpose) flour
1 pound skinless white fish fillets, sliced thickly

1 Preheat oven to 425°F.
2 Combine milk and garlic in large saucepan; bring almost to the boil. Season. Add potato; simmer, stirring occasionally, about 15 minutes or until potato is tender. Drain over large heatproof bowl; reserve milk mixture.
3 Melt butter in large frying pan; cook onion, stirring, until soft. Add flour; cook, stirring, about 2 minutes or until mixture bubbles and thickens. Gradually stir in reserved milk; cook, stirring, until mixture boils and thickens. Stir in potato.
4 Divide half the potato mixture into six 1-cup shallow ovenproof dishes; top with fish, then remaining potato mixture. Bake, uncovered, about 15 minutes or until fish is cooked.

prep + cook time 50 minutes serves 6
nutritional count per serving 13.1g total fat (7.9g saturated fat); 345 cal; 29.3g carbohydrate; 25.7g protein; 3.2g fiber

notes A mandolin or V-slicer is ideal for thinly slicing potatoes. As you need the starch from the potatoes in this recipe, don't rinse them after slicing. To stop them turning brown, add them to the hot milk and garlic as soon as they are sliced.
We used two large dishes here – each will serve three.

spicy sardine and spaghetti bake

8	ounces spaghetti
1	cup breadcrumbs
⅓	cup finely chopped fresh flat-leaf parsley
⅓	cup olive oil
10	ounces canned sardines in oil, drained
8	ounces cherry tomatoes, chopped coarsely
4	cloves garlic, crushed
1½	teaspoons dried chili flakes

1 Preheat oven to 425°F.

2 Cook pasta in large saucepan of boiling water until tender; drain, reserve ⅓ cup cooking liquid.

3 Combine breadcrumbs, parsley and 1 tablespoon of the oil in medium bowl.

4 Heat remaining oil in same pan; cook sardines, tomato, garlic and chili, stirring, until tomato begins to soften. Stir in pasta; season to taste.

5 Spoon mixture into 8-cup ovenproof dish; pour over reserved cooking liquid. Sprinkle with breadcrumb mixture. Bake, uncovered, about 10 minutes or until browned lightly.

prep + cook time 30 minutes **serves** 4

nutritional count per serving 29.7g total fat (6.1g saturated fat); 598 cal; 56.3g carbohydrate; 24g protein; 4.6g fiber

note Seasoning a dish with pepper when it already contains chili isn't doubling up, as they both have distinct flavors.

shrimp and feta with crispy filo

1 tablespoon olive oil
1 large onion, chopped finely
1 medium red bell pepper, sliced thinly
2 garlic cloves, crushed
1 cup bottled tomato sauce
½ cup water
½ teaspoon dried oregano
¼ teaspoon dried chili flakes
2 pounds uncooked medium shrimp
3 ounces soft feta cheese, crumbled
8 sheets filo pastry
1½ ounces butter, melted

1 Preheat oven to 425°F.
2 Heat oil in large frying pan; cook onion and pepper, stirring, until onion softens. Add garlic; cook, stirring, until fragrant. Add sauce, the water, oregano and chili; simmer, uncovered, until sauce thickens slightly. Season to taste.
3 Transfer tomato mixture to 6-cup ovenproof dish. Shell and devein shrimp; stir into tomato mixture. Sprinkle with cheese; bake, uncovered, 10 minutes.
4 Meanwhile, stack four sheets of pastry, brushing with butter between each layer. Roll pastry stack loosely; cut roll into thick strips. Repeat with remaining pastry. Loosen pastry rolls with fingers; sprinkle randomly over shrimp mixture. Bake, uncovered, about 15 minutes or until browned lightly.

prep + cook time 40 minutes **serves** 4
nutritional count per serving 21.2g total fat (10.2g saturated fat); 447 cal; 27.1g carbohydrate; 35.4g protein; 3.5g fiber

note We've used medium pans here – each pan will serve two. Use pans that have ovenproof handles, or wrap regular handles in several layers of foil to protect them from the heat of the oven.

smoked haddock potato bake

1 pound potatoes
2½ ounces butter
1 medium onion, chopped finely
2 stalks celery, trimmed, sliced thinly
2 tablespoons plain (all-purpose) flour
1 cup fish stock
1 pound smoked haddock, skinned, chopped coarsely
1 cup frozen peas
½ cup cream
2 tablespoons coarsely chopped fresh flat-leaf parsley

1 Preheat oven to 425°F.
2 Boil, steam or microwave potatoes until almost tender; drain. When cool enough to handle, slice thinly.
3 Meanwhile, melt 1½ ounces of the butter in large saucepan; cook onion and celery, stirring, until onion softens. Add flour; cook, stirring, about 2 minutes or until mixture bubbles and thickens. Gradually stir in stock; cook, stirring, until mixture boils and thickens. Remove from heat; stir in fish, peas, cream and parsley. Season to taste.
4 Spoon mixture into shallow 6-cup ovenproof dish; top with potato. Brush with remaining melted butter. Bake, uncovered, about 25 minutes or until browned lightly.

prep + cook time 50 minutes **serves** 6
nutritional count per serving 19.7g total fat (12.5g saturated fat); 342 cal; 15.6g carbohydrate; 24.1g protein; 3.6g fiber

notes We used desiree potatoes in this recipe. Season this dish carefully as the haddock and stock are already salty.

salmon bread and butter pudding

8 large slices white bread, crusts removed
1½ ounces butter, softened
4½ ounces piece hot-smoked salmon, flaked
4 eggs
2 cups milk
1 cup cream
2 tablespoons finely chopped fresh chives
2 teaspoons finely chopped fresh tarragon
1 tablespoon dijon mustard
½ cup coarsely grated cheddar cheese

1 Preheat oven to 400°F. Grease 8-cup ovenproof dish.
2 Spread both sides of bread with butter; cut into triangles. Layer bread, slightly overlapping, in dish; sprinkle with salmon.

3 Whisk eggs, milk, cream, chives, tarragon, mustard and half the cheese in medium bowl until combined; season. Pour half the egg mixture over bread. Stand 1 hour.
4 Pour remaining egg mixture into dish; sprinkle with remaining cheese. Place ovenproof dish in large baking dish. Add enough hot water to baking dish to come halfway up the sides of ovenproof dish. Cover loosely with foil; bake 25 minutes. Uncover; bake about 20 minutes or until set. Remove pudding from baking dish. Stand 5 minutes before serving.

prep + cook time 1 hour (+ standing) **serves** 4
nutritional count per serving 56.5g total fat (32.8g saturated fat); 909 cal; 64.3g carbohydrate; 35.3g protein; 3.8g fiber

spicy tuna pasta bake

9½ ounces cannelloni tubes
2 tablespoons olive oil
3 cloves garlic, crushed
4 drained anchovy fillets, chopped finely
2 cups bottled tomato sauce
½ cup seeded kalamata olives, halved
2 tablespoons finely chopped fresh oregano
1 tablespoon rinsed, drained capers
½ teaspoon dried chili flakes
13½ ounces canned tuna in oil, drained, flaked
¼ cup coarsely grated mozzarella cheese
¼ cup finely grated parmesan cheese

1 Preheat oven to 425°F.
2 Cook pasta in large saucepan of boiling water until tender; drain, reserving ¼ cup of cooking liquid.
3 Meanwhile, heat oil in large saucepan; cook garlic and anchovy, stirring, until fragrant. Stir in sauce, olives, oregano, capers and chili; simmer, uncovered, 5 minutes. Season to taste. Stir in pasta, tuna and the reserved cooking liquid.
4 Spoon mixture into 8-cup ovenproof dish; sprinkle with combined cheeses. Bake, uncovered, about 15 minutes or until browned lightly.

prep + cook time 35 minutes **serves** 4
nutritional count per serving 26.5g total fat (5.3g saturated fat); 653 cal; 66g carbohydrate; 34.6g protein; 6g fiber

sardine, potato and lemon bake

¼ cup olive oil
2 pounds potatoes, peeled, sliced thinly
1 tablespoon honey
1 tablespoon finely chopped preserved lemon rind
1 teaspoon harissa paste
10 fresh sardine fillets

1 Preheat oven to 425°F.
2 Heat oil in large frying pan; cook potato, in batches, stirring, about 10 minutes or until browned lightly. Drain oil from potato over medium heatproof bowl; stir honey, rind and harissa into bowl, season.
3 Layer potato and sardines in 6-cup ovenproof dish. Pour honey mixture into dish. Bake, uncovered, about 20 minutes or until sardines are cooked.

prep + cook time 40 minutes **serves** 4
nutritional count per serving 23.9g total fat (4.6g saturated fat); 454 cal; 32.6g carbohydrate; 25.3g protein; 3.4g fiber

note A mandolin or V-slicer is ideal to quickly slice potatoes evenly. Rinse the sliced potato in cold water to remove the starch and avoid the slices sticking together during cooking. Drain slices, then pat dry with paper towels before cooking.

tuna and corn bake

6½ ounces rigatoni pasta
1½ ounces butter
1½ tablespoons plain (all-purpose) flour
2½ cups hot milk
1½ cups coarsely grated cheddar cheese
13½ ounces canned corn kernels, drained
13½ ounces canned tuna in water, drained, flaked
1 cup frozen peas
2 scallions, chopped finely
2 tablespoons finely chopped fresh flat-leaf parsley
2 tablespoons lemon juice

1 Preheat oven to 425°F.
2 Cook pasta in large saucepan of boiling water until tender; drain.
3 Meanwhile, melt butter in medium saucepan. Add flour; cook, stirring, about 2 minutes or until mixture bubbles and thickens. Gradually stir in milk; cook, stirring, until sauce boils and thickens. Stir in pasta, ⅓ cup of the cheese, corn, tuna, peas, scallion, parsley and juice; season to taste.
4 Spoon mixture into 8-cup ovenproof dish; sprinkle with remaining cheese. Bake, uncovered, about 25 minutes or until browned lightly.

prep + cook time 40 minutes **serves** 6
nutritional count per serving 22.8g total fat (13.9g saturated fat); 503 cal; 41.2g carbohydrate; 31.2g protein; 4.5g fiber

This is a take on the Russian coulibiac salmon pie. It's important to season each element (rice, fish and swiss chard). Choose a fish fillet approximately the same length as the dish. To check if the salmon is cooked, insert a knife through the center of the pie and check its temperature on your wrist; it should feel hot.

salmon, swiss chard and rice pie

¼ cup olive oil
1 large onion, chopped finely
1½ cups jasmine rice
2¼ cups water
2 eggs
2 pounds swiss chard, trimmed
1 pound skinless salmon fillet
2 cloves garlic, crushed
⅓ cup heavy cream
1 sheet puff pastry

1 Heat 2 tablespoons of the oil in medium saucepan; cook onion, stirring, until soft. Add rice; stir to coat in onion mixture. Add the water; bring to the boil. Reduce heat to medium-low; cook, covered, about 13 minutes or until water is absorbed and rice is tender. Transfer rice mixture to parchment-paper-lined oven tray to cool.

2 Meanwhile, boil eggs in small saucepan of water for 6 minutes. Drain; rinse under cold water. Shell and halve eggs.

3 Preheat oven to 425°F. Grease shallow 5-cup square ovenproof dish.

4 Heat large frying pan; cook swiss chard, stirring, until wilted. Remove from pan. When cool enough to handle, squeeze excess liquid from swiss chard; chop coarsely.

5 Season salmon. Heat remaining oil in same pan; cook salmon on both sides until browned. Remove from pan. Add swiss chard and garlic to same pan; cook, stirring, until fragrant. Stir in cream; season to taste.

6 Spread half the rice in dish; cover with half the swiss chard. Top with salmon; place eggs along center of salmon, cover with remaining swiss chard to form a slight dome; cover with remaining rice. Cut pastry to fit dish; cover with pastry, tucking edges inside dish. Bake, uncovered, about 30 minutes or until browned lightly.

prep + cook time 1 hour 10 minutes serves 6
nutritional count per serving 28.7g total fat (6.9g saturated fat); 589 cal; 53.7g carbohydrate; 26.8g protein; 4.5g fiber

chicken

chicken and eggplant parmigiana

2 chicken breast fillets
2 tablespoons olive oil
1 medium eggplant, sliced thinly
4 trimmed medium swiss chard leaves
1⅔ cups bottled tomato pasta sauce
1 cup coarsely grated mozzarella cheese
⅓ cup finely grated parmesan cheese

1 Preheat oven to 425°F.
2 Cut chicken breasts in half horizontally. Combine chicken and half the oil in large bowl. Cook chicken on heated oiled grill plate (or grill or barbecue) until browned both sides. Place in oiled 6-cup ovenproof dish.

3 Cook eggplant on heated oiled grill plate (or grill or barbecue), brushing with remaining oil, until browned and tender.
4 Meanwhile, boil, steam or microwave swiss chard about 30 seconds or until just tender; transfer to bowl of iced water. Drain; squeeze excess water from swiss chard. Drain on paper towels.
5 Top chicken with swiss chard and eggplant, then sauce; sprinkle with combined cheeses. Bake, uncovered, about 20 minutes or until browned lightly.

prep + cook time 45 minutes serves 4
nutritional count per serving 20.2g total fat (6.7g saturated fat); 372 cal; 10.5g carbohydrate; 34.9g protein; 5.4g fiber

serving suggestion Serve with a green salad.

chicken, sausage and bean cassoulet

2 pounds chicken pieces
½ cup plain (all-purpose) flour
¼ cup olive oil
10 pork chipolata sausages
1 medium onion, chopped coarsely
1 large carrot, chopped coarsely
2 cloves garlic, sliced thinly
4 sprigs fresh thyme
1 bay leaf
2 tablespoons tomato paste
1½ pounds canned diced tomatoes
1 cup chicken stock
1¾ pounds canned white beans, rinsed, drained
1 cup breadcrumbs
2 tablespoons finely chopped fresh flat-leaf parsley

1 Preheat oven to 400°F.
2 Coat chicken in flour; shake off excess. Heat half the oil in large flameproof casserole dish; cook chicken, in batches, until browned. Remove from dish.
3 Cook sausages, in same dish until browned. Remove from dish.
4 Heat remaining oil in same dish; cook onion, carrot, garlic, thyme and bay leaf, stirring, until onion softens. Add paste; cook, stirring, 1 minute. Return chicken and sausages to dish with undrained tomatoes and stock; bring to the boil. Cover; bake 20 minutes. Remove from oven; stir in beans. Cover; bake 30 minutes or until sauce thickens and chicken is tender. Season to taste. Preheat grill (broiler).
5 Sprinkle cassoulet with combined breadcrumbs and parsley; place under grill until browned lightly.

prep + cook time 1 hour 25 minutes serves 8
nutritional count per serving 26.2g total fat (7.7g saturated fat); 420 cal; 21.6g carbohydrate; 22.6g protein; 5g fiber

chicken cacciatore with gremolata and parmesan topping

3 pounds chicken pieces
⅓ cup plain (all-purpose) flour
2 tablespoons olive oil
1 large red onion, chopped coarsely
2 cloves garlic, crushed
1 medium red bell pepper, sliced thickly
½ cup dry white wine
13 ounces canned diced tomatoes
13 ounces canned cherry tomatoes in tomato juice
½ cup chicken stock
2 tablespoons tomato paste
1 teaspoon superfine sugar
½ cup pitted black olives

GREMOLATA AND PARMESAN TOPPING
½ cup coarsely grated parmesan cheese
⅓ cup finely chopped fresh flat-leaf parsley
1 tablespoon finely grated lemon rind
1 clove garlic, crushed

1 Preheat oven to 400°F.
2 Coat chicken in flour; shake off excess. Heat oil in large deep flameproof casserole dish; cook chicken, in batches, until browned. Remove from dish.
3 Cook onion, garlic and pepper in same dish, stirring, until onion softens. Add wine; simmer, uncovered, until liquid is reduced by half. Stir in undrained tomatoes, stock, paste and sugar.
4 Return chicken to dish; bring to the boil. Cover; bake 45 minutes. Uncover; bake about 45 minutes or until chicken is tender and sauce has thickened. Skim fat from surface; stir in olives. Season to taste.
5 Meanwhile, make gremolata and parmesan topping. Sprinkle over dish just before serving.

GREMOLATA AND PARMESAN TOPPING Combine ingredients in a small bowl.

prep + cook time 1 hour 50 minutes serves 6
nutritional count per serving 29.1g total fat (8.6g saturated fat); 483 cal; 19g carbohydrate; 31.4g protein; 3.8g fiber

serving suggestion Serve with steamed rice or cooked pasta of your choice.

chicken and sweet corn bake

3	cups coarsely chopped barbecued chicken
13½	ounces canned creamed corn
1½	cup coarsely grated cheddar cheese
½	cup cream
4	scallions, sliced thinly
1	cup breadcrumbs

1 Preheat oven to 425°F.

2 Combine chicken, corn, cheese, cream and scallion in large bowl; season. Spoon mixture into four oiled 1-cup ovenproof dishes; sprinkle with breadcrumbs.

3 Place dishes on oven tray; bake about 20 minutes or until browned lightly.

note You need to buy a large barbecued chicken to get the amount of shredded meat required for this recipe.

prep + cook time 25 minutes **serves** 4

nutritional count per serving 26.9g total fat (14.4g saturated fat); 480 cal; 27.2g carbohydrate; 30.4g protein; 5.1g fiber

cheesy chicken, tomato and bacon rigatoni

10 ounces rigatoni pasta
2 tablespoons olive oil
1 pound chicken tenderloins, sliced thinly
1 medium red onion, sliced thinly
4 rindless bacon slices, chopped coarsely
2 cups bottled tomato sauce
¼ cup finely chopped fresh basil
1½ cups coarsely grated cheddar cheese

1 Preheat oven to 425°F.
2 Cook pasta in large saucepan of boiling water until tender; drain. Return to pan.
3 Meanwhile, heat half the oil in large frying pan; cook chicken until browned. Remove from pan.
4 Heat remaining oil in same pan; cook onion and bacon, stirring, until bacon is crisp. Return chicken to pan with sauce; simmer, uncovered, 10 minutes. Stir in basil; season.
5 Stir chicken mixture and half the cheese into pasta. Spoon pasta mixture into 8-cup ovenproof dish; sprinkle with remaining cheese. Bake, uncovered, about 15 minutes or until browned lightly.

prep + cook time 50 minutes **serves** 4
nutritional count per serving 34.9g total fat (14g saturated fat); 847 cal; 65.8g carbohydrate; 64g protein; 6g fiber

81

mexican chicken tortilla bake

1 tablespoon olive oil
1 large red onion, sliced thinly
1 medium red bell pepper, sliced thinly
1½ pounds canned diced tomatoes
13½ ounces canned kidney beans, rinsed, drained
10 ounces canned corn kernels, rinsed, drained
1 ounce taco seasoning
2 cups shredded barbecued chicken
⅓ cup coarsely chopped fresh cilantro
7½-inch flour tortillas
¾ cup coarsely grated mozzarella cheese

1 Preheat oven to 425°F.
2 Heat oil in large saucepan; cook onion and pepper, stirring, until tender. Add undrained tomatoes, beans, corn and seasoning; simmer, uncovered, about 10 minutes or until thickened slightly. Add chicken and cilantro; cook, stirring, until hot. Season to taste.
3 Line base and sides of 8-inch springform pan with foil or parchment paper; place on oven tray. Line base of pan with a tortilla; top with one-third of the chicken mixture. Repeat layering with remaining tortillas and chicken mixture, finishing with a tortilla; sprinkle with cheese. Bake, uncovered, about 20 minutes until browned lightly. Stand 5 minutes before cutting.

prep + cook time 45 minutes **serves** 6
nutritional count per serving 13.2g total fat (3.9g saturated fat); 376 cal; 33.8g carbohydrate; 26.4g protein; 8.1g fiber

serving suggestion Serve with an avocado salad or guacamole.
note You need to buy half large barbecued chicken to get the amount of shredded meat required for this recipe.

spicy chicken and ratatouille pilaf

2 tablespoons olive oil
1 medium red onion, chopped coarsely
3 cloves garlic, sliced thinly
4 medium tomatoes, chopped coarsely
2 medium zucchini, chopped coarsely
1 medium eggplant, chopped coarsely
1 medium red bell pepper, chopped coarsely
1 cup bottled tomato sauce
1 pound chicken tenderloins, sliced thinly
1 fresh long red chili, chopped finely
1 cup basmati rice
1½ cups chicken stock
¼ cup loosely packed fresh basil leaves

1 Preheat oven to 400°F.
2 Combine all ingredients, except basil, in 10-cup ovenproof dish. Cover tightly with foil; bake 50 minutes, stirring occasionally, or until rice is tender.
3 Stand, covered, 10 minutes; season to taste. Serve sprinkled with basil.

prep + cook time 1 hour 10 minutes **serves** 4
nutritional count per serving 9g total fat (1.5g saturated fat); 342 cal; 36.9g carbohydrate; 25.2g protein; 5.3g fiber

tip Using a round or oval dish will help the rice to cook more evenly, square corners attract the heat from the oven, which can cause the rice in the corners to dry out.

chicken, zucchini and mushroom lasagna

⅓ cup olive oil
1 medium onion, chopped finely
2 cloves garlic, crushed
1 pound ground chicken
2 tablespoons tomato paste
13 ounces canned diced tomatoes
1 teaspoon superfine sugar
⅓ cup coarsely chopped fresh basil
3 medium zucchini, sliced thinly
5 flat mushrooms, sliced thinly
12 ounces fresh lasagna sheets
⅓ cup finely grated parmesan cheese

WHITE SAUCE
2 ounces butter
¼ cup plain (all-purpose) flour
2¼ cups hot milk
⅓ cup finely grated parmesan cheese

1 Preheat oven to 400°F.
2 Heat 1 tablespoon of the oil in medium saucepan; cook onion and garlic, stirring, until onion softens. Add chicken; stir until browned. Add paste, undrained tomatoes and sugar; bring to the boil. Reduce heat; simmer, uncovered, 5 minutes. Stir in basil; season.

3 Cook zucchini and mushrooms, in batches, on heated oiled grill plate (or grill or barbecue), brushing with remaining oil, until browned and tender.
4 Meanwhile, make white sauce.
5 Line base of 8-cup ovenproof dish with lasagna sheets, trimming to fit. Top with one-third of the chicken mixture, half the vegetable mixture and half the white sauce. Top with lasagna sheets, trimming to fit. Top with half the remaining chicken mixture, remaining vegetable mixture, lasagna sheets, then remaining chicken mixture. Top with remaining lasagna sheets and remaining white sauce; sprinkle with cheese.
6 Cover dish with foil; bake 20 minutes. Uncover; bake about 30 minutes or until browned lightly. Stand 10 minutes before serving.

WHITE SAUCE Melt butter in medium saucepan. Add flour; cook, stirring, 2 minutes. Remove from heat; gradually stir in milk. Cook, stirring, until sauce boils and thickens. Simmer, uncovered, 3 minutes. Season to taste. Remove from heat; stir in cheese.

prep + cook time 1 hour 15 minutes serves 6
nutritional count per serving 34.8g total fat (13.4g saturated fat); 696 cal; 59.8g carbohydrate; 34.4g protein; 6.6g fiber

serving suggestion Serve with a mixed green salad.

red curry chicken risotto

1 tablespoon peanut oil
1 pound chicken thigh fillets, chopped coarsely
1 medium onion, chopped finely
1 medium red bell pepper, chopped coarsely
1 fresh long red chili, sliced thinly
3 cloves garlic, crushed
1½ cups arborio rice
¼ cup red curry paste
2 cups chicken stock
½ cup water
4 kaffir lime leaves, sliced thinly
1 cup coconut cream
4 ounces green beans, trimmed, halved
1 ounce baby spinach leaves, chopped coarsely
¼ cup loosely packed fresh cilantro leaves

1 Preheat oven to 400°F.
2 Heat oil in large flameproof casserole dish; cook chicken until browned. Remove from dish.
3 Heat remaining oil in same dish; cook onion, pepper, chili and garlic, stirring, until onion softens. Add rice and paste; cook, stirring, 1 minute.
4 Return chicken to dish with stock, the water and lime leaves. Cover with foil; bake about 50 minutes, stirring occasionally, or until rice is tender. Remove from oven; stir in coconut cream, beans and spinach. Cover; stand 10 minutes. Season to taste; serve sprinkled with cilantro.

prep + cook time 1 hour 15 minutes **serves** 4
nutritional count per serving 32.6g total fat (15.4g saturated fat); 713 cal; 68.7g carbohydrate; 33.8g protein; 5.5g fiber

note Use whatever type of curry paste you prefer.

creamy chicken, bacon and corn chowder

1½ ounces butter
 2 rindless bacon slices, chopped finely
 1 medium leek, sliced thinly
 2 stalks celery, trimmed, chopped finely
 1 medium carrot, chopped finely
 ¼ cup plain (all-purpose) flour
 2 cups hot milk
 ½ cup cream
 2 medium potatoes, chopped coarsely
 1 fresh bay leaf
 2 chicken breast fillets, chopped coarsely
10 ounces canned corn kernels, rinsed, drained
 2 tablespoons finely chopped fresh chives
6½ ounces crusty bread, cut into small cubes

1 Preheat oven to 400°F.
2 Melt butter in large saucepan; cook bacon, leek, celery and carrot, stirring, until vegetables soften. Add flour; cook, stirring, 1 minute. Gradually stir in milk and cream; stir in potato and bay leaf. Cook, stirring, until mixture boils and thickens. Simmer, uncovered, about 5 minutes or until potato is tender. Stir in chicken, corn and chives.
3 Spoon mixture into 8-cup ovenproof dish; sprinkle with bread. Bake, uncovered, about 30 minutes or until browned lightly.

prep + cook time 1 hour serves 6
nutritional count per serving 21.8g total fat (12.5g saturated fat); 496 cal; 42.1g carbohydrate; 30g protein; 6.1g fiber

note Discard bay leaf before serving.

chicken biryani with cauliflower and peas

¼ cup yogurt
2 cups Indian butter chicken simmer sauce
1 pound chicken thigh fillets, trimmed, chopped coarsely
1½ cups basmati rice
2 tablespoons vegetable oil
2½ cups cauliflower florets
1 large onion, sliced thinly
3 cloves garlic, crushed
1½-inch piece fresh ginger, grated
1 fresh long green chili, sliced thinly
1 tablespoon garam masala
4 cloves
2 teaspoons ground turmeric
3 cups chicken stock
½ cup frozen peas, thawed
⅓ cup dried currants
¼ cup loosely packed fresh cilantro leaves

1 Combine yogurt, ¼ cup of the simmer sauce and chicken in large bowl. Cover; refrigerate 1 hour.
2 Preheat oven to 400°F.
3 Rinse rice under cold water until water runs clear; drain. Heat half the oil in large flameproof casserole dish; cook cauliflower, stirring, about 5 minutes or until browned lightly and tender. Remove from pan.
4 Heat remaining oil in same dish; cook onion, stirring, until browned lightly. Add chicken; cook, stirring, until browned. Add garlic, ginger, chili and spices; cook, stirring, about 1 minute or until fragrant. Add rice; cook, stirring, 1 minute. Stir in stock. Cover; bake about 45 minutes or until rice is tender and liquid absorbed.
5 Remove dish from oven; add cauliflower, peas and currants. Cover, stand for 10 minutes. Fluff rice with a fork; season to taste.
6 Bring remaining simmer sauce to the boil in small saucepan. Serve biryani topped with heated simmer sauce, cilantro leaves and some extra yogurt, if you like.

prep + cook time 1 hour 15 minutes (+ refrigeration) serves 4
nutritional count per serving 32.1g total fat (9.9g saturated fat); 780 cal; 84.7g carbohydrate; 35.1g protein; 7.5g fiber

chicken stroganoff with potato topping

4 medium potatoes, chopped coarsely
½ cup milk
2 ounces butter
1 pound chicken thigh fillets, sliced thinly
¼ cup plain (all-purpose) flour
2 tablespoons olive oil
1½ ounces butter, extra
1 large onion, sliced thinly
2 cloves garlic, crushed
6 ounces button mushrooms, sliced thinly
2 teaspoons sweet paprika
⅓ cup dry white wine
1 cup chicken stock
1 tablespoon worcestershire sauce
¼ cup tomato paste
½ cup light sour cream
2 tablespoons finely chopped fresh flat-leaf parsley

1 Preheat oven to 425°F.
2 Boil, steam or microwave potato until tender; drain. Mash potato with milk and butter in large bowl until smooth.
3 Meanwhile, coat chicken in flour; shake off excess. Heat oil in large saucepan; cook chicken until browned. Remove from pan.
4 Melt extra butter in same pan; cook onion, garlic and mushrooms, stirring, until vegetables soften. Add paprika; cook, stirring, about 1 minute or until fragrant. Add wine and stock; simmer, uncovered, until liquid is reduced by half. Return chicken to pan with sauce, paste and sour cream; bring to the boil. Remove from heat; stir in parsley. Season to taste.
5 Spoon chicken mixture into 10-cup ovenproof dish. Top with potato; roughen surface with a fork. Bake, uncovered, about 30 minutes or until browned lightly.

prep + cook time 1 hour serves 6
nutritional count per serving 31.7g total fat (15.4g saturated fat); 491 cal; 24.9g carbohydrate; 22.8g protein; 3.9g fiber

red wine and rosemary chicken with polenta crust

8 chicken thigh fillets, halved
2 tablespoons plain (all-purpose) flour
1 teaspoon cracked black pepper
2 tablespoons olive oil
4 ounces ham, chopped coarsely
8 shallots, halved
1 large carrot, chopped coarsely
4 cloves garlic, sliced thinly
2 sprigs rosemary
1 cup dry red wine
1 cup chicken stock
2 tablespoons tomato paste
½ cup coarsely grated mozzarella cheese

POLENTA CRUST
1 cup chicken stock
1 cup milk
½ cup polenta

1 Preheat oven to 400°F.
2 Coat chicken in combined flour and pepper; shake off excess.
3 Heat oil in large frying pan; cook chicken, in batches, until browned. Remove from pan.
4 Cook ham, shallots, carrot and garlic in same pan, stirring, until browned lightly. Return chicken to pan with rosemary, wine, stock and paste; bring to the boil. Season. Spoon mixture into six 1-cup ovenproof dishes; bake, covered, 20 minutes.
5 Meanwhile, make polenta crust.
6 Spread polenta crust mixture over chicken mixture; sprinkle with cheese. Bake, uncovered, about 20 minutes or until browned lightly. Stand 10 minutes before serving.

POLENTA CRUST Bring stock and milk to the boil in small saucepan; gradually stir in polenta. Reduce heat; simmer, stirring, about 10 minutes or until polenta thickens.

prep + cook time 1 hour 40 minutes serves 6
nutritional count per serving 34.7g total fat (11.9g saturated fat); 711 cal; 30.4g carbohydrate; 61.5g protein; 2.6g fiber

note If ham is unavailable, use three chopped bacon slices.

meat

lamb shank shepherd's pie

4 french-trimmed lamb shanks
⅓ cup plain (all-purpose) flour
2 tablespoons olive oil
8 baby onions, peeled
1 large carrot, chopped coarsely
4 cloves garlic, sliced thinly
2 tablespoons each fresh thyme and rosemary leaves
½ cup dry white wine
1¼ cups chicken stock
1¼ cups water
2 pounds potatoes, chopped coarsely
1½ ounces butter
½ cup hot milk

CREAMED SPINACH
1 tablespoon olive oil
1 ounce butter
1 small onion chopped finely
2 cloves garlic, crushed
2 pounds spinach, trimmed
½ cup cream
pinch ground nutmeg

1 Preheat oven to 400°F.
2 Coat lamb in flour; shake off excess. Heat half the oil in large flameproof casserole dish; cook lamb until browned. Remove from dish.
3 Heat remaining oil in same dish; cook onions, carrot, garlic and herbs, stirring, until onions are browned lightly. Add wine; boil, uncovered, until liquid is evaporated. Return lamb to dish with stock and the water; bring to the boil. Cover dish tightly with foil; bake about 2 hours or until lamb is tender.
4 Meanwhile, boil, steam or microwave potato until tender; drain. Mash potato in medium bowl with butter and hot milk until smooth. Season to taste. Make creamed spinach.
5 Remove dish from oven; discard lamb shank bones. Break meat into large chunks; return meat to dish. Combine potato and spinach in large bowl; spoon over lamb mixture. Bake, uncovered, about 30 minutes or until browned lightly.

CREAMED SPINACH Heat oil and butter in large frying pan; cook onion and garlic, stirring, until onion softens. Add spinach, in batches, stirring, until wilted and liquid is evaporated. Add cream and nutmeg; simmer about 3 minutes or until thickened slightly. Season to taste.

prep + cook time 2 hours 50 minutes serves 6
nutritional count per serving 38.4g total fat (18.4g saturated fat); 616 cal; 30.8g carbohydrate; 29.5g protein; 8.8g fiber

beef stew with chive dumplings

2 pounds beef chuck steak, chopped coarsely
2 tablespoons plain (all-purpose) flour
2 tablespoons olive oil
½ ounce butter
1 medium onion, chopped coarsely
2 cloves garlic, crushed
1 medium parsnip, chopped coarsely
1 medium carrot, chopped coarsely
1 cup dry red wine
1½ cups beef stock
2 tablespoons tomato paste
4 sprigs fresh thyme

CHIVE DUMPLINGS
1 cup self-raising flour
2 ounces butter, chopped finely
1 egg, beaten lightly
¼ cup coarsely grated parmesan cheese
¼ cup finely chopped fresh chives
¼ cup milk, approximately

1 Preheat oven to 350°F.
2 Coat beef in flour; shake off excess. Heat oil in large flameproof baking dish; cook beef, in batches, until browned. Remove from dish.
3 Melt butter in same dish; cook onion, garlic, parsnip and carrot, stirring, until onion softens. Add wine; cook, stirring, until liquid reduces by half. Return beef to dish with stock, paste and thyme; bring to the boil. Season. Cover; bake 1¾ hours.
4 Meanwhile, make chive dumplings.
5 Remove dish from oven. Drop rounded tablespoons of dumpling mixture, about ¾ inch apart, on top of stew. Bake, uncovered, about 25 minutes or until dumplings are browned lightly.

CHIVE DUMPLINGS Place flour in medium bowl; rub in butter. Stir in egg, cheese, chives and enough milk to make a soft sticky dough.

prep + cook time 2 hours 20 minutes serves 4
nutritional count per serving 47.7g total fat (19.7g saturated fat); 918 cal; 42.3g carbohydrate; 67.5g protein; 5.1g fiber

baked meatballs

2 pounds ground beef
2 eggs
1 cup packaged breadcrumbs
½ cup finely grated parmesan cheese
⅓ cup finely chopped fresh flat-leaf parsley
¼ cup olive oil
1 medium onion, chopped finely
2 cloves garlic, crushed
2⅔ cups bottled tomato sauce
1½ pounds canned crushed tomatoes
1 cup frozen peas
½ cup coarsely chopped fresh basil
6½ ounces ricotta cheese
½ cup finely grated parmesan cheese, extra

1 Preheat oven to 400°F. Oil 12-cup ovenproof dish.
2 Combine beef, eggs, breadcrumbs, parmesan and parsley in large bowl; season. Using wet hands, roll rounded tablespoons of mixture into balls.
3 Heat half the oil in large frying pan; cook meatballs, in batches, until browned all over. Transfer to dish.
4 Heat remaining oil in same pan; cook onion and garlic, stirring, until onion softens. Remove from heat; stir in sauce, undrained tomatoes, peas and basil; season. Pour tomato mixture over meatballs; top with crumbled ricotta and extra parmesan. Bake, uncovered, about 40 minutes or until meatballs are cooked through.

prep + cook time 1 hour 10 minutes **serves** 6
nutritional count per serving 34.3g total fat (13.4g saturated fat); 632 cal; 27.3g carbohydrate; 50.9g protein; 7.1g fiber

serving suggestion Serve with pasta or crusty bread and a green salad.

osso bucco with polenta crust

8 pieces veal osso bucco
⅓ cup plain (all-purpose) flour
2 tablespoons olive oil
1 ounce butter
1 large onion, chopped finely
1 large carrot, chopped finely
1 stalk celery, chopped finely
4 cloves garlic, crushed
½ cup dry white wine
1½ pounds canned crushed tomatoes
2 sprigs fresh rosemary
1 cup chicken stock
1 tablespoon finely chopped fresh flat-leaf parsley
2 teaspoons finely grated lemon rind

POLENTA CRUST
2 cups milk
2 cups water
1 cup instant polenta
½ cup finely grated parmesan cheese
1 egg, beaten lightly

1 Preheat oven to 400°F.
2 Coat veal in flour; shake off excess. Heat half the oil and butter in large flameproof baking dish; cook veal, in batches, until browned. Remove from dish.
3 Heat remaining oil and butter in same dish; cook onion, carrot, celery and garlic, stirring, until onion softens. Add wine; boil, uncovered, until liquid has evaporated. Return veal to dish with undrained tomatoes, rosemary and stock; bring to the boil. Season. Cover tightly with foil; bake 1½ hours.
4 Meanwhile, make polenta crust.
5 Remove dish from oven; discard veal bones and rosemary. Break meat into large chunks. Divide veal mixture among eight oiled 1¼-cup ovenproof dishes; top with polenta crust mixture. Place dishes on oven tray; bake, uncovered, about 25 minutes or until browned lightly. Serve sprinkled with combined parsley and rind.

POLENTA CRUST Combine milk and the water in medium saucepan; bring almost to the boil. Gradually stir in polenta, cook, stirring, about 5 minutes or until thickened. Remove from heat, stir in cheese and egg; season to taste.

prep + cook time 2 hours 20 minutes serves 8
nutritional count per serving 15.3g total fat (6.3g saturated fat); 408 cal; 26.7g carbohydrate; 36.5g protein; 3.4g fiber

note We used larger dishes here – each will serve four.

salami antipasto pasta

12 ounces large shell pasta
6½ ounces shaved salami, chopped coarsely
⅓ cup drained sun-dried tomatoes
9 ounces bottled char-grilled vegetables, drained, chopped coarsely
2⅔ cups bottled tomato sauce
2 cups water
⅓ cup each coarsely chopped fresh basil and flat-leaf parsley
1 cup coarsely grated mozzarella cheese

1 Preheat oven to 400°F. Oil 10-cup baking dish.
2 Combine pasta, salami, tomatoes, vegetables, sauce, the water and chopped herbs in dish; season lightly.
3 Cover dish with foil; bake 50 minutes, stirring halfway through cooking. Remove from oven; sprinkle with cheese. Bake, uncovered, about 20 minutes or until pasta is tender.

prep + cook time 1 hour 20 minutes **serves** 6
nutritional count per serving 19.5g total fat (6.8g saturated fat); 502 cal; 57.5g carbohydrate; 21.3g protein; 5.7g fiber

notes We have deliberately used dried, uncooked pasta in this dish. The texture of the final dish is a little chewy, but still tender.
We cooked this recipe in two ovenproof dishes – each dish will serve three.

veal goulash with parsley dumplings

2 tablespoons olive oil

1½ ounces butter

2 pounds veal shoulder, chopped coarsely

1 large red bell pepper, chopped coarsely

1 large onion, chopped coarsely

2 cloves garlic, crushed

2 tablespoons tomato paste

1 tablespoon plain (all-purpose) flour

1 tablespoon sweet paprika

2 teaspoons caraway seeds

½ teaspoon cayenne pepper

1½ cups beef stock

½ cup water

2 tablespoons coarsely chopped fresh flat-leaf parsley

¼ cup finely grated parmesan cheese

PARSLEY DUMPLINGS

1 cup self-raising flour

2 ounces butter, chopped finely

1 egg, beaten lightly

⅓ cup finely chopped fresh flat-leaf parsley

¼ cup finely grated parmesan cheese

¼ cup milk, approximately

1 Preheat oven to 350°F.

2 Heat half the oil and butter in large flameproof casserole dish; cook veal, in batches, until browned. Remove from dish.

3 Heat remaining oil and butter in same dish; cook pepper, onion and garlic, stirring, until vegetables soften. Add paste, flour, paprika, caraway and cayenne; cook, stirring, 1 minute. Return veal to dish with stock and the water; bring to the boil. Cover; bake 1½ hours.

4 Meanwhile, make parsley dumplings.

5 Remove dish from oven; stir in parsley. Season to taste. Drop rounded tablespoons of the dumpling mixture, about ¾ inch apart, on top of goulash; sprinkle dumplings with cheese. Bake, uncovered, about 20 minutes or until dumplings are cooked through.

PARSLEY DUMPLINGS Place flour in medium bowl; rub in butter. Stir in egg, parsley, cheese and enough milk to make a soft sticky dough.

prep + cook time 2 hours 20 minutes serves 4
nutritional count per serving 42.7g total fat (20.2g saturated fat); 800 cal; 35.7g carbohydrate; 67g protein; 3.7g fiber

pork sausage cassoulet

2 teaspoons olive oil
8 thick pork sausages
1 large onion, chopped finely
5 ounces piece pancetta, chopped finely
1 medium carrot, chopped coarsely
1 stalk celery, trimmed, chopped coarsely
2 cloves garlic, crushed
2 tablespoons tomato paste
1½ cups chicken stock
13 ounces canned crushed tomatoes
1 teaspoon fennel seeds
12½ ounces canned white beans, rinsed, drained
2 thick slices sourdough bread
1 tablespoon coarsely chopped fresh flat-leaf parsley

1 Preheat oven to 400°F.
2 Heat oil in large flameproof casserole dish; cook sausages, until browned. Drain sausages on paper towels, chop coarsely.
3 Cook onion, pancetta, carrot, celery and garlic in same dish, stirring, until onion softens. Add paste; cook, stirring, 1 minute. Return sausages to dish with stock, undrained tomatoes, fennel seeds and beans; bring to the boil. Bake, uncovered, 30 minutes.
4 Preheat grill (broiler). Season cassoulet to taste. Top with chunks of sourdough; grill until browned lightly. Sprinkle with parsley.

prep + cook time 1 hour 10 minutes **serves** 6
nutritional count per serving 41.6g total fat (16.2g saturated fat); 578 cal; 20.2g carbohydrate; 28.8g protein; 6.2g fiber

egg and bacon pie

5 sheets filo pastry
1½ ounces butter, melted
4 rindless bacon slices, chopped finely
6 eggs
⅔ cup milk
¾ cup coarsely grated cheddar cheese

1 Preheat oven to 400°F. Oil 8-inch springform tin; place on oven tray.
2 Brush one sheet of filo pastry with some of the melted butter; fold in half, then ease into base and side of tin. Repeat with remaining pastry and melted butter, to completely cover base and side of tin.
3 Cook bacon in heated oiled frying pan until crisp; drain on paper towels. Combine eggs and milk in large bowl; season.
4 Place bacon and half the cheese in tin; pour in egg mixture. Sprinkle with remaining cheese. Roll down edges of pastry until touching egg mixture; bake, uncovered, about 45 minutes or until set. Stand 10 minutes before serving.

prep + cook time 1 hour 10 minutes serves 4
nutritional count per serving 32.5g total fat (16.6g saturated fat); 470 cal; 12.4g carbohydrate; 32.5g protein; 0.7g fiber

chorizo and chickpea stew

2 tablespoons olive oil
2 cured chorizo sausages, sliced thickly
2 medium onions, sliced thinly
1 tablespoon light brown sugar
2 teaspoons cumin seeds
1 teaspoon ground cilantro
1½ pounds canned crushed tomatoes
1½ pounds canned chickpeas, rinsed, drained
1 cup salt-reduced chicken stock
½ cup raisins
2 ounces baby spinach leaves

1   Preheat oven to 400°F.
2   Heat half the oil in large baking dish; cook chorizo, stirring, until browned. Remove from dish. Add onion and sugar to same dish; cook, stirring occasionally, over medium heat, about 15 minutes or until onion is lightly caramelized. Add spices; cook, stirring, 1 minute.
3   Return chorizo to dish with undrained tomatoes, chickpeas, stock and raisins; bring to the boil. Cover; bake 40 minutes. Remove from oven; stir in spinach. Season to taste.

prep and cook time 1 hour 10 minutes **serves** 6
nutritional count per serving 25.5g total fat (7.4g saturated fat); 443 cal; 31.8g carbohydrate; 19.3g protein; 7.5g fiber

beef ragu cannelloni

2 tablespoons olive oil
1 stalk celery, trimmed, chopped finely
1 small brown onion, chopped finely
1 small carrot, chopped finely
2 fresh long red chilies, chopped finely
1 clove garlic, crushed
1½ ounce piece pancetta, chopped finely
8 ounces ground beef
6½ ounces ground pork
⅓ cup dry white wine
¾ cup milk
1 cup chicken stock
13 ounces canned diced tomatoes
2 tablespoons tomato paste
2⅓ cups heavy cream
¾ cup finely grated parmesan cheese
8 ounces fresh cannelloni sheets

1 Heat half the oil in medium saucepan; cook celery, onion, carrot, chili and garlic, stirring, until onion softens. Add pancetta; cook, stirring, 3 minutes. Remove from pan.
2 Heat remaining oil in same pan; cook beef and pork, stirring, until browned. Return pancetta mixture to pan with wine; boil, uncovered, until reduced by half. Add milk; bring to the boil. Boil, uncovered, until reduced by half. Add stock, undrained tomatoes and paste; bring to the boil. Reduce heat; simmer, uncovered, about 1 hour 10 minutes or until thickened. Season to taste. Cool 20 minutes.
3 Preheat oven to 400°F. Oil shallow 14-cup ovenproof dish.
4 Combine cream and cheese in large bowl; season. Spread 1 cup of the cream mixture over base of dish.
5 Carefully tear each cannelloni sheet into three pieces. Place ¼ cup of beef mixture along one short side of each piece; roll to enclose. Place cannelloni, seam-side down, into dish; pour remaining cream mixture over cannelloni. Cover with foil; bake 30 minutes. Uncover; bake about 15 minutes or until browned lightly. Stand 5 minutes before serving.

prep + cook time 2 hours 15 minutes (+ cooling)
serves 6
nutritional count per serving 54.3g total fat (30.3g saturated fat); 741 cal; 31.7g carbohydrate; 28.9g protein; 3.4g fiber

sweet and sour meatballs

2 pounds ground beef
2 eggs
1 cup packaged breadcrumbs
1 tablespoon finely chopped fresh flat-leaf parsley
¼ cup olive oil
1 large red bell pepper, chopped coarsely
1 large onion, chopped coarsely
1 large carrot, chopped coarsely
2 stalks celery, trimmed, chopped coarsely

SWEET AND SOUR SAUCE
14 ounces canned pineapple pieces in natural juice
2 tablespoons cornstarch
2 tablespoons light soy sauce
¾ cup water
⅔ cup white vinegar
⅓ cup ketchup
3 teaspoons superfine sugar

1 Preheat oven to 400°F. Oil 12-cup ovenproof dish.
2 Make sweet and sour sauce.
3 Combine beef, eggs, breadcrumbs and parsley in large bowl; season. Using wet hands, roll rounded tablespoons of beef mixture into balls.
4 Heat half the oil in large frying pan; cook meatballs, in batches, until browned. Transfer to dish. Heat remaining oil in same pan; cook pepper, onion, carrot and celery, stirring, until onion softens. Add sweet and sour sauce; bring to the boil. Remove from heat; stir in reserved pineapple pieces.
5 Pour vegetable mixture over meatballs in dish. Cover dish with foil; bake 30 minutes. Uncover; bake about 10 minutes or until meatballs are cooked.

SWEET AND SOUR SAUCE Drain pineapple through sieve into large bowl; reserve juice. Blend cornstarch with soy sauce in medium bowl; add juice, the water, vinegar, ketchup and sugar. Season.

prep + cook time 1 hour serves 6
nutritional count per serving 24.1g total fat (8.1g saturated fat); 514 cal; 31.9g carbohydrate; 39.8g protein; 3.9g fiber

serving suggestion Serve with steamed jasmine rice.

lamb and eggplant pot pies with feta crust

2 tablespoons olive oil
1 large eggplant, peeled, chopped coarsely
1 large onion, chopped finely
4 cloves garlic, crushed
2 pounds ground lamb
1 teaspoon ground cinnamon
½ teaspoon ground allspice
1½ cups beef stock
2 tablespoons tomato paste
¼ cup finely grated parmesan cheese
2 tablespoons each finely chopped fresh mint and oregano

FETA CRUST
1½ pounds potatoes, chopped coarsely
1 ounce butter
¼ cup hot milk
6½ ounces feta cheese, crumbled

1 Heat half the oil in large saucepan; cook eggplant, stirring, until tender. Remove from pan. Heat remaining oil in same pan; cook onion and garlic, stirring, until onion softens. Add lamb; cook, stirring, until browned. Add spices; cook, stirring, 1 minute. Add stock and paste; bring to the boil. Reduce heat; simmer, uncovered, about 20 minutes or until thickened slightly. Remove from heat; stir in parmesan, herbs and eggplant.
2 Meanwhile, make feta crust.
3 Preheat oven to 400°F. Oil six 1-cup ovenproof dishes; place on oven trays.
4 Divide lamb mixture among dishes; top with feta crust. Bake, uncovered, about 30 minutes or until browned lightly.

FETA CRUST Boil, steam or microwave potato until tender; drain. Mash potato in medium bowl with butter and milk until smooth. Stir in feta; season to taste.

prep and cook time 1 hour 10 minutes serves 6
nutritional count per serving 32.3g total fat (15.3g saturated fat); 560 cal; 19g carbohydrate; 46.4g protein; 4.5g fiber

sausage risotto

1 tablespoon olive oil
6 thick beef sausages
1 medium onion, chopped finely
¼ cup firmly packed fresh basil leaves
2 cloves garlic, crushed
2 cups arborio rice
2 tablespoons tomato paste
½ cup dry white wine
2⅔ cups bottled tomato sauce
2½ cups water
2 teaspoons superfine sugar
2 ounces baby arugula leaves

1 Preheat oven to 350°F.
2 Heat oil in large flameproof casserole dish; cook sausages, in batches, until browned. Remove from dish; cut into thirds.
3 Cook onion, basil and garlic in same dish, stirring, until onion softens. Add rice and paste; stir to coat rice in onion mixture. Add wine; bring to the boil. Boil, uncovered, stirring until liquid is absorbed. Stir in sauce, the water and sugar; bring to the boil. Season.
4 Cover dish with foil; bake 25 minutes, stirring halfway through cooking. Uncover; stir in sausages. Bake about 10 minutes or until rice is tender. Stir in arugula.

prep + cook time 1 hour **serves** 6
nutritional count per serving 43.5g total fat (18.9g saturated fat); 789 cal; 68.7g carbohydrate; 24.6g protein; 8g fiber

glossary

ALLSPICE also called jamaican pepper or pimento; tastes like a combination of nutmeg, cumin, clove and cinnamon. Sold whole or ground.

ARUGULA also called rugula and rucola; peppery green leaf eaten raw in salads or used in cooking. Baby arugula is smaller and less peppery.

BALSAMIC VINEGAR made from the juice of Trebbiano grapes; has a deep rich brown color and a sweet and sour flavor.

BEAN SPROUTS tender new growths of assorted beans and seeds germinated for consumption as sprouts.

BEANS
broad also called fava, windsor and horse beans; available dried, fresh, canned and frozen. Fresh should be peeled twice (discarding both the outer long green pod and the beige-green tough inner shell); the frozen beans have had their pods removed but the beige shell still needs removal.
kidney medium-size red bean, slightly floury in texture yet sweet in flavor; sold dried or canned, it's found in bean mixes and is used in chili con carne.
white a generic term we use for canned or dried cannellini, haricot, navy or great northern beans, all of which can be substituted for each other.

BELL PEPPER also called pepper. Discard seeds and membranes before use.

BREADCRUMBS
fresh bread, usually white, processed into crumbs.
japanese also called panko; available in two kinds: larger pieces and fine crumbs; they have a lighter texture than Western-style breadcrumbs. Available from Asian food stores and some supermarkets.
packaged prepared fine-textured but crunchy white breadcrumbs; good for coating foods that are to be fried.
stale crumbs made by grating or processing one- or two-day-old bread.

CAPERS the grey-green buds of a warm climate (usually Mediterranean) shrub, sold either dried and salted or pickled in a vinegar brine; tiny young ones, called baby capers, are also available both in brine or dried in salt. All capers should be rinsed before using.

CARAWAY SEEDS small dried seed from a member of the parsley family; has a sharp anise flavor.

CAYENNE PEPPER a thin-fleshed, long, extremely hot dried red chilli, usually purchased ground.

CHEESE
blue mould-treated cheeses mottled with blue veining. Varieties include firm and crumbly stilton types and mild, creamy brie-like cheeses.
cheddar semi-hard, yellow to off-white, sharp-tasting cheese.
feta Greek in origin; a crumbly textured goat- or sheep-milk cheese having a sharp, salty taste. Ripened and stored in salted whey; particularly good cubed and tossed into salads.
gorgonzola a creamy Italian blue cheese with a mild, sweet taste; good as an accompaniment to fruit or used to flavor sauces (especially pasta).
gruyère a hard-rind Swiss cheese with small holes and a nutty, slightly salty flavor. Popular for soufflés.
mozzarella soft, spun-curd cheese; originating in southern Italy where it was traditionally made from water-buffalo milk. Now generally made from cow's milk, it's a popular pizza cheese because of its low melting point and elasticity when heated.
parmesan also known as parmigiano, parmesan is a hard, grainy cow's-milk cheese that originated in the Parma region of Italy. The curd is salted in brine for a month before being aged for up to two years in humid conditions.
pizza cheese a commercial blend of varying proportions of processed grated mozzarella, cheddar and parmesan.
ricotta a soft, sweet, moist, white cow's-milk cheese with a low fat content (8.5%) and a slightly grainy texture. The name roughly translates as "cooked again" and refers to ricotta's manufacture from a whey that is itself a by-product of cheese making.

CHICKPEAS also called garbanzos, hummus or channa; an irregularly round, sandy-colored legume. Has a firm texture even after cooking, a floury mouth-feel and robust nutty flavor; available canned or dried (reconstitute for several hours in water before use).

CHIPOLATA SAUSAGES also known as "little fingers"; highly spiced, coarse-textured beef sausage.

CHORIZO SAUSAGE of Spanish origin, made of coarsely ground pork and highly seasoned with garlic and chilli. They are deeply smoked, very spicy and dry-cured. Also available raw (fresh).

CILANTRO also called pak chee or chinese parsley; bright-green-leafed herb with both pungent aroma and taste. Used as an ingredient in a wide variety of cuisines. Coriander seeds are dried and sold either whole or ground, and neither form tastes remotely like the fresh leaf, so should not be substituted.

COCONUT
cream obtained commercially from the first pressing of the coconut flesh alone, without the addition of water.
milk not the liquid found inside the fruit, which is called coconut water, but the diluted liquid from the second pressing of the white flesh of a mature coconut (the first pressing produces coconut cream).

CORNSTARCH Available made from wheat (wheaten cornstarch gives a lighter texture in cakes), or 100% corn (maize); used as a thickening agent in cooking.

CREAM we use fresh cream, also known as pure or pouring cream, unless otherwise stated. Has no additives. Minimum fat content 35%.
sour a thick, commercially cultured sour cream with a minimum fat content of 35%; light sour cream has 18.5% fat.
double a dolloping cream with a minimum fat content of 45%.
heavy a whipping cream containing a thickener. Minimum fat content 35%.

CUMIN also known as zeera or comino; resembling caraway in size, cumin is the dried seed of a plant related to the parsley family. Its spicy, almost curry-like flavor is essential to the traditional foods of Mexico, India, North Africa and the Middle East. Also available ground.

DIJON MUSTARD also called french mustard. A pale brown, creamy, fairly mild mustard.

DRIED CURRANTS tiny, almost black raisins so-named after a grape variety that originated in Corinth, Greece.

EGGPLANT also called aubergine. Ranging in size from tiny to very large and in color from pale green to deep purple. Can also be purchased char-grilled, packed in oil, in jars.

EGGS we use large chicken eggs weighing an average of 2 oz. unless stated otherwise in the recipes in this book. If a recipe calls for raw or barely cooked eggs, exercise caution if there is a salmonella problem in your area, particularly in food eaten by children and pregnant women.

FENNEL also called finocchio or anise; a crunchy green vegetable slightly resembling celery that's eaten raw in salads, fried as an accompaniment, or used as an ingredient in soups and sauces. Also the name given to the dried seeds of the plant, which have a stronger licorice flavor.

FLOUR

plain also known as all-purpose; unbleached wheat flour is the best for baking: the gluten content ensures a strong dough, producing a light result.

self-raising all-purpose plain or wholemeal flour with baking powder and salt added; make yourself with plain flour sifted with baking powder in the proportion of 1 cup flour to 2 teaspoons baking powder.

GARAM MASALA literally meaning blended spices in its northern Indian place of origin; based on varying proportions of cardamom, cinnamon, cloves, coriander, fennel and cumin, roasted and ground together. Black pepper and chili can be added.

GHEE a semifluid clarified butter

HARISSA a North African paste made from dried red chilies, garlic, olive oil and caraway

seeds; can be used as a rub for meat, an ingredient in sauces and dressings, or eaten as a condiment. It is available from Middle Eastern food shops and some supermarkets.

HORSERADISH a vegetable with edible green leaves but mainly grown for its long, pungent white root. Occasionally found fresh in specialty greengrocers and some Asian food shops, but commonly purchased in bottles at the supermarket in two forms: prepared horseradish and horseradish cream. These cannot be substituted one for the other in cooking but both can be used as table condiments. Horseradish cream is a commercially prepared creamy paste consisting of grated horseradish, vinegar, oil and sugar, while prepared horseradish is preserved grated root.

KAFFIR LIME LEAVES also known as bai magrood and looks like two glossy dark green leaves joined end to end, forming a rounded hourglass shape. Sold fresh, dried or frozen, the dried leaves are less potent so double the number if using them as a substitute for fresh; a strip of fresh lime peel may be substituted for each kaffir lime leaf.

KECAP MANIS a dark, thick sweet soy sauce used in most South-East Asian cuisines. Depending on the manufacturer, the sauce's sweetness is derived from the addition of either molasses or palm sugar when brewed.

KUMARA the Polynesian name of an orange-fleshed sweet potato often confused with yam.

LEEKS a member of the onion family, the leek resembles a green onion but is much larger and more subtle in flavor. Tender baby or pencil leeks can be eaten whole with minimal cooking but adult leeks are usually trimmed of most of the green tops then chopped or sliced and cooked.

MARINARA MIX a mixture of uncooked, chopped seafood available from many major supermarkets, as well as fishmarkets and fishmongers.

MUSHROOMS

button small, cultivated white mushrooms with a mild flavor. When a recipe calls for

an unspecified type of mushroom, use button.

flat large, flat mushrooms with a rich earthy flavor, ideal for filling and barbecuing. They are sometimes misnamed field mushrooms, which are wild mushrooms.

swiss brown also known as roman or cremini. Light to dark brown mushrooms with full-bodied flavor; suited for use in casseroles or being stuffed and baked.

MUSTARD SEEDS

black also known as brown mustard seeds; more pungent than the white variety.

white also known as yellow mustard seeds; used ground for mustard powder and in most prepared mustards.

OSSO BUCCO another name used by butchers for veal shin, usually cut into 1¼- to 2-inch-thick slices and used in the slow-cooked casserole of the same name.

PANCETTA an Italian unsmoked bacon; pork belly is cured in salt and spices then rolled into a sausage shape and dried for several weeks.

PAPRIKA ground dried sweet red bell pepper; many grades and types are available, including sweet, hot, mild and smoked.

PARCHMENT PAPER also known as baking parchment; a silicone-coated paper that is used for lining baking pans and oven trays so cakes and biscuits won't stick, making removal easy.

PINE NUTS also known as pignoli; not a nut but a small, cream-colored kernel from pine cones. Best roasted before use to bring out the flavor.

POLENTA also known as cornmeal; a flour-like cereal made of dried corn (maize). Also the dish made from it.

PRESERVED LEMON whole or quartered salted lemons preserved in a mixture of water, or olive oil, and lemon juice. Occasionally spices such as cinnamon, clove and coriander are added. Available from delicatessens and specialty food shops. Use the rind only and rinse well before using.

RAISINS dried sweet grapes (traditionally muscatel grapes).

RED CURRY PASTE probably the most popular thai curry paste; a hot blend of different flavors that complements the richness of pork, duck and seafood, also works well in marinades and sauces.

RICE

arborio small, round-grain rice well-suited to absorb a large amount of liquid; the high level of starch makes it especially suitable for risottos, giving the dish its classic creaminess.

basmati a white, fragrant long-grained rice; the grains fluff up beautifully when cooked. It should be washed several times before cooking.

jasmine or thai jasmine, is a long-grained white rice recognized around the world for its perfumed aromatic quality, moist texture and the fact that it clings together after cooking. Jasmine rice is sometimes substituted for basmati rice.

ROLLED OATS flattened oat grain rolled into flakes and traditionally used for porridge. Instant oats are also available for a speedy breakfast, but use traditional oats for baking.

SCALLION also known as green onion or, incorrectly, shallot; an immature onion picked before the bulb has formed, with a long, bright-green edible stalk.

SHALLOTS also called french shallots, golden shallots or eschalots. Small and elongated, with a brown skin, they grow in tight clusters similar to garlic.

SMOKED HADDOCK smoked fish that has a white flesh and a milky smoky flavor; the skin is orange colored.

SNOW PEA SPROUTS shoots of the snow pea (mange tout) plant. Available from supermarkets or greengrocers.

SOY SAUCE also known as sieu; made from fermented soya beans. Several types are available in supermarkets and Asian food stores. We use japanese soy sauce in our recipes unless otherwise indicated.

dark soy deep brown, almost black in color; rich, with a thicker consistency than other types. Pungent, though not particularly salty, it is good for marinating.

japanese soy an all-purpose low-sodium soy sauce made with more wheat content than its Chinese counterparts; fermented in barrels and aged. Possibly the best table soy and the one to choose if you only want one variety.

light soy a fairly thin, pale but salty tasting sauce; used in dishes in which the natural color of the ingredients is to be maintained. Not to be confused with salt-reduced or low-sodium soy sauces.

SPECK smoked pork.

SPINACH also known as english spinach and, incorrectly, silver beet. Baby spinach leaves are best eaten raw in salads; the larger leaves should be added last to soups, stews and stir-fries, and should be cooked until barely wilted.

SWISS CHARD also known as silver beet and, incorrectly, spinach; has fleshy stalks and large leaves, both of which can be prepared as for spinach.

TACO SEASONING MIX a packaged seasoning meant to duplicate the mild Mexican sauce made from oregano, cumin, chilies and other spices.

TOMATOES

bottled tomato sauce a prepared tomato-based sauce (sometimes called ragu or sugo on the label); comes in varying degrees of thickness and levels of spicing.

canned whole peeled tomatoes in natural juices; available crushed, chopped or diced. Use undrained.

cherry also known as tiny tim or tom thumb tomatoes; a small, round tomato.

egg also called plum or roma, these are smallish, oval-shaped tomatoes much used in Italian cooking or salads.

paste triple-concentrated tomato puree.

puree canned pureed tomatoes (not tomato paste); substitute with fresh peeled and pureed tomatoes.

sauce also known as ketchup or catsup; a flavored condiment made from tomatoes, vinegar and spices.

semi-dried partially dried tomato pieces in olive oil; softer and juicier than sun-dried, these are not a preserve therefore do not keep as long as sun-dried.

sun-dried tomato pieces that have been dried with salt; this dehydrates the tomato and concentrates the flavor. We generally use sun-dried tomatoes packaged in oil, unless otherwise specified.

truss small vine-ripened tomatoes with vine still attached.

TORTILLA thin, round unleavened bread originating in Mexico; available frozen, fresh or vacuum-packed. Two kinds of tortilla are available, one made from wheat flour and the other from corn.

TURMERIC also called kamin; is a rhizome related to galangal and ginger. Must be grated or pounded to release its acrid aroma and pungent flavor; known for the golden color it imparts. Ground turmeric can be substituted for the less common fresh turmeric (use 2 teaspoons of ground turmeric plus a teaspoon of sugar for every ¾ ounce of fresh turmeric called for in a recipe).

WORCESTERSHIRE SAUCE a dark colored thin condiment made from garlic, soy sauce, tamarind, onions, molasses, lime, anchovies, vinegar and seasonings. Available in supermarkets.

ZUCCHINI also known as courgette; small, pale- or dark-green, yellow or white vegetable belonging to the squash family. Harvested when young, its edible flowers can be stuffed with a mild cheese then deep-fried or oven-baked to make a delicious appetizer.

conversion chart

MEASURES

All cup and spoon measurements are level. The most accurate way of measuring dry ingredients is to weigh them. When measuring liquids, use a clear glass or plastic jug with the metric markings.

We use large eggs with an average weight of 2 oz.

DRY MEASURES

STANDARD	METRIC
½oz	15g
1oz	30g
2oz	60g
3oz	90g
4oz (¼lb)	125g
5oz	155g
6oz	185g
7oz	220g
8oz (½lb)	250g
9oz	280g
10oz	315g
11oz	345g
12oz (¾lb)	375g
13oz	410g
14oz	440g
15oz	470g
16oz (1lb)	500g
24oz (1½lb)	750g
32oz (2lb)	1kg

LIQUID MEASURES

STANDARD	METRIC
1 fluid oz	30ml
3 fluid oz	100ml
4 fluid oz	125ml
5 fluid oz	150ml
6 fluid oz	190ml
8 fluid oz	250ml
10 fluid oz	300ml
16 fluid oz	500ml
20 fluid oz	600ml
1¾ pints	1000ml (1 litre)

LENGTH MEASURES

STANDARD	METRIC
⅛in	3mm
¼in	6mm
½in	1cm
¾in	2cm
1in	2.5cm
2in	5cm
2½in	6cm
3in	8cm
4in	10cm
5in	13cm
6in	15cm
7in	18cm
8in	20cm
9in	22cm
10in	25cm
11in	28cm
12in (1ft)	30cm

OVEN TEMPERATURES

The oven temperatures in this book are for conventional ovens; if you have a convection or fan-forced oven, decrease the temperature by 10-20 degrees.

	°F (FAHRENHEIT)	°C (CELSIUS)
Very slow	250	120
Slow	300	150
Moderately slow	325	160
Moderate	350	180
Moderately hot	400	200
Hot	425	220
Very hot	475	240

index

STERLING
New York

An Imprint of Sterling Publishing
387 Park Avenue South
New York, NY 10016

ISBN 978-1-4549-1017-6

Distributed in Canada by Sterling Publishing
c/o Canadian Manda Group, 165 Dufferin Street
Toronto, Ontario, Canada M6K 3H6

For information about custom editions, special sales, and premium and corporate purchases,
please contact Sterling Special Sales at 800-805-5489 or specialsales@sterlingpublishing.com.

Manufactured in China

2 4 6 8 10 9 7 5 3 1

www.sterlingpublishing.com